# How to Supervise People

*Techniques for Getting Results through Others*

By
Donald P. Ladew

CAREER PRESS
3 Tice Road, P. O. Box 687
Franklin Lakes, NJ 07417
1-800-CAREER-1; 201-848-0310 (NJ and outside U.S.)
FAX: 201-848-1727

HOW TO SUPERVISE PEOPLE
Cover design by Barry Littman
Printed in the U.S.A. by Book-mart Press

To order this title, please call toll-free 1-800-CAREER-1 (NJ and Canada: 201-848-0310) to order using VISA or MasterCard, or for further information on books from Career Press.

## Library of Congress Cataloging-in-Publication Data

Ladew, Donald P.
    How to supervise people : techniques for getting results through others / Donald P. Ladew.
        p.    cm.
    Rev. ed. of: The supervisor's handbook. c1998
    Includes index.
    ISBN 1-56414-363-5 (pbk.)
    1. Supervision of employees--Handbooks, manuals, etc.   I. Title.
HF5549.12.L33    1998
658.3'02--dc21                                    98-10418

# Contents

# Introduction

What does it take to be a successful supervisor? Some people believe you've got to be Mr. Nice Guy to get ahead in management. Others say you've got to play the part of the Wicked Witch to keep employees in line. Choose either role, and you'll find yourself going home every evening with a sick stomach, wondering where you went wrong.

The truth is, you don't have to be a dictator to supervise effectively, nor do you have to be a pal to everyone in order to get people on your side. Most important, being stressed out doesn't have to be part of your job!

What you *do* need to succeed as a supervisor are solid skills. When "experts" talk about management as an art, don't believe it. It doesn't require extraordinary charisma, magic or a special set of genes. It requires skill—and like any skill, effective supervision can be learned.

If you carefully study people who are exceptional supervisors, you'll see that each of them is following a path that many have walked before. They're following clearly defined steps that have been proven to work. They've learned to apply methods and techniques that work and avoid those that fail. These are the things that you can learn, too.

This handbook contains everything you need to become an excellent supervisor. It's filled with practical ideas to handle the situations you're most likely to encounter. It has dozens of tips that will help you get the most not only from yourself, but from the people you supervise as well.

Study it to sharpen your managerial skills, then keep it close at hand as your trusted desk reference.

When the concepts you learn in this book are combined with your desire and enthusiasm to succeed, you'll have the winning formula for achieving your professional goals and for becoming an exceptional supervisor.

We are confident that this handbook can play a role in helping you handle the most common challenges you face as a supervisor. While the guidelines and techniques presented here are suggestions and not meant to supersede your organization's policies, government regulations or your own good judgment, you should experiment with these concepts. Try new things. Let the ideas in this handbook serve as a springboard for your own creativity as a supervisor, and watch your effectiveness soar!

# Chapter 1

# Supervision and Leadership

## What you'll learn:

- What it takes to be a leader.
- How to get off to a good start as a supervisor.
- How to gain power through delegating.

Supervisors are members of the management team who oversee the work of others and act as intermediaries between management and employees.

However, as we all know, doing these things doesn't necessarily make you successful in your role as a supervisor. In order to succeed, you need to do more. You must understand what enables one supervisor to be successful, while others are either mediocre or, worse, failures.

If you were to study supervisors, you would soon see that successful supervisors are leaders. In their leadership role, they coach, nurture and empower others to use their skills, expertise and ideas to produce results. As leaders, they inspire increased efficiency, productivity, initiative, ownership and creativity by providing direction, acknowledgment, challenges and support. In short, great supervisors succeed by leading others to success.

This ability isn't something you're born with. Indeed, many people who have been described as "born leaders" showed little indication of their leadership in their early years. Many were poor students or were even identified by others as having substandard intelligence or skills.

There is, however, a common thread in the history of all leaders—whether they became presidents, CEOs or supervisors. They were all willing to study the subject of leadership and to continue studying as they moved on to greater and greater responsibilities. They discovered leadership is something they could learn. And so can you!

## To Manage or to Lead?

The first critical question to ask yourself when you become a supervisor is whether you're going to manage the people who report to you or lead them. Study after study shows you get the best results when you manage assets and lead people. The corporate countryside is littered with failed companies that thought a successful business is built on management—that leadership takes care of itself. Leadership must come first. That means you must know how to be a leader before you can succeed as a supervisor.

## Qualities of Effective Leaders

Effective leaders have three essential qualities:

1. **Leaders inspire trust.** They inspire confidence that they will act in the best interests of those who follow them and that they will serve the needs of the group without sacrificing the rights of the individual. A leader displays a sense of rightness. A leader knows when to proceed and when to pause, when to criticize and when to praise. Most important, a leader knows how to encourage others to excel.

2. **Leaders know how to follow.** The ability to lead involves being both a leader and a follower. Leaders realize they can't know all the answers. They respect followers who listen to what they say and, when appropriate, allow them to take the lead.

3. **Leaders make contact.** Leaders know they can't lead from behind the comfort of their desks. Issuing memos may be all right for routine activities, but when problems arise, leaders must be in the trenches, making things happen.

---

Take a minute and think of a supervisor you admire, then answer the following questions:

1. How does the supervisor you admire rate as a leader?


2. If this person has been your supervisor, how important have his or her leadership skills been to you and your ability to accomplish your work? In what ways?


3. Which of this person's leadership qualities would you like to incorporate into your supervisory style?


4. What leadership qualities do you already have that you would want to emphasize in your role as a supervisor?

---

# How You Demonstrate Your Leadership

Following are ways that you can apply these basic qualities to your role as a supervisor and a leader.

## 1. Be an advocate for the people who report to you.

When you lead others, you stand up for the people you supervise. If someone has a complaint about one of your people, you handle the problem. You don't permit others to bypass your responsibility or authority. You're loyal to your employees, and you speak up for them when someone threatens their ability to accomplish their tasks.

## 2. Be fair without playing favorites or being a "pal."

In addition to supervising your team, you're also a voice for those above you in the managerial chain. An effective leader can't be both manager and "one of the gang." It's far better to strive for an even temper, fairness and a full understanding of what it is you're asking others to do.

## 3. Create a great work environment.

As a supervisor, you can't create pride or a willingness among employees to do a good job. Those qualities have to come from the people who do the work. What you can create, however, is an environment where the natural pride a worker feels for a job well done can flourish.

Dr. W. Edwards Deming, the father of Total Quality Management and the man for whom Japan's highest quality prize is named, said in his famous 14 Points: "The aim of supervision should be to help people, machines and gadgets do a better job."

You create an environment that helps your staff do a better job when you:

- Let employees help improve processes.
- Ask employees what prevents them from doing their jobs.
- Ask management for the tools your people need.

Creating an environment where people can take pride in themselves and their work generates positive energy in the workplace. Physics teaches us there are two kinds of energy: potential and kinetic. Potential energy is stored like a battery, and kinetic energy is in motion, like a freight train moving down the track. There's a third parameter to energy called inertia, a resistance to change in the kind of energy being expended. If you apply these three concepts to the workplace, they would look like this:

### *Potential Energy = New Ideas*
*Characterized by people who say,*
*"I'm willing to try new things."*

### *Kinetic Energy = Ideas in Motion*
*Characterized by people who say,*
*"Let's work together to make this happen."*

### *Inertia = Resistance to Change*
*Characterized by people who say,*
*"I've seen it all."*

The supervisor is the catalyst who gets the ball rolling, recognizes potential, overcomes objections and gets people to give their best. In your company, there are great untapped sources of potential energy waiting for someone to overcome the inertia and convert it to kinetic energy. That someone could be you!

## 4. Provide stability during times of change.

One of your responsibilities as a supervisor is to give your staff a sense of stability, especially during times of change. This is particularly true in the modern business environment.

You can't prevent change, nor should you want to. However, anything you can do to enhance your staff's ability to feel more in control of the future will create stability. To provide more stability for yourself and your employees you must:

- Take steps to prevent unwanted surprises.

- Consult your staff before you make changes.

- Maintain communication with your superiors.

- Learn as much about your job as possible.

- Plan for the short term as well as the long.

## 5. You must have courage.

When you become a supervisor, you become part of a group of other managers. Individuals who make tough decisions head on stand out in this group.

You will succeed if you focus on doing the right thing. There is real satisfaction in making these decisions. It is how a supervisor grows, and it is also how your peers and seniors judge your readiness to move up the ladder and gain greater responsibility. The way you handle your current duties determines how much responsibility you will be given tomorrow. Your ability to handle work issues is an indicator of your potential for your career and your company's growth.

Reflect upon the following questions and determine how you can tap your staff's potential.

1. Your manager asks you how to do a task you do well. How do you feel? What do you want to do?

2. You're responsible for an important project. How do you feel? Compare that feeling with the one you have when you're asked to take responsibility for something that you know isn't very important.

3. You want to do a good job, but the tools you're expected to work with are substandard. When you point this out to your manager, he tells you to make do with what you have. How do you feel about the job now?

4. Your manager makes a lot of promises, but never follows through. How do you feel about working for this person? How much effort do you want to put into doing a good job?

One of the most common complaints workers have about their jobs is that management doesn't value their opinions.

The following types of people may have the potential to spark new energy in your department if you're willing to listen to their ideas.

1. **The quiet workers who always get the job done.** People have different ways of communicating. Sometimes it's easy to overlook the quiet people who can always be counted on to get the job done. Show them you value their contributions and ask them what they think could be done to improve efficiency. They're probably just waiting for someone to ask!

2. **The angry workers who complain all the time.** Often people who complain are either ignored or thought of as an irritation. However, if they are complaining about the procedures or conditions in your department, they may be vocalizing things others are too afraid to mention. Put these people on the spot. Ask them how they would solve the problems and then put them in charge of making things better. Channel their anger into constructive action.

3. **The status quo workers who don't want to "rock the boat."** People who have adopted this mentality may be the hardest of all to inspire, but it can be done. Take a gentle approach with them. Realize their caution comes from the fear of losing their jobs if they make waves. Put them in situations where they must take small risks and reward them by supporting their efforts and encouraging confidence in themselves and you.

# Dealing with the "System" Like a Leader

The "system"—also known as "the way things are done around here"—can either be positive and reinforcing, or it can put seemingly immovable obstacles in the way of the work your staff needs to do. All too often, the system poses challenges comparable to that faced by the Greek Sisyphus, who was condemned by the gods to roll a rock up a steep mountain forever, only to have it immediately roll down again when he reached the top.

When the system interferes with your employees' work, they generally are powerless to change the system or even get around it. An effective supervisor doesn't blame the worker when the system raises too many barriers to doing a good job. To find fault with their efforts when the system limits their production, quality or cycle times is a sure route to failure as a supervisor.

As a leader, there are things you can do to deal with the system. For example, instead of complaining about the system, think about how you can change it so your employees can get their jobs done more efficiently. Following is an example of how to do this:

*Jan, a purchasing supervisor at a medium-sized company, was told to cut costs. However, when she studied where she could cut costs, she made an amazing discovery. A significant amount of time and money was wasted on the procedures that management had said to follow.*

*Purchase orders for items as small as a box of papers clips cost an average of $230 dollars to process because the system required that seven executives sign off on each purchase order. The average time to process each order was nine working days!*

*Instead of complaining, Jan decided to do something about it. She persuaded the company to issue corporate credit cards, each with a $1,000 limit, and give them to employees who most frequently purchased low-cost items. After that, all employees had to do was call the local office-supply business, place an order, and provide the credit card number. The materials usually arrived the same day, the bank handled the paperwork, and the company got one monthly bill.*

*The result? Huge savings for the company.*

No matter how forward-thinking your company is, there will always be barriers to what you want to do. There will always be procedures that have outlived their effectiveness. Management will always make decisions that don't necessarily serve your department's best interests.

As a supervisor and leader, don't complain about these things. Complaining never accomplished any goals. Find an area where the system is bogging down your employees, and then work to change it. Create a win-win situation for both your employees and your company.

# Be a Leader from the Start

The impressions you make the first days on the job will greatly determine your success in the weeks ahead.

Following are "Supervisor Basics" that every supervisor should use to get off to a good start.

## 1. Make yourself known.

Personally meet every person on your team. Make frequent visits during the first few weeks on your new post. Really listen for employees' concerns and take notes.

## 2. Don't try to change everything at once.

It's best if you make very few changes when you're new. If you make changes too quickly, people feel you don't value them or their work. Remember, before you can operate a machine, you have to know how it works. When a new supervisor attempts to change things too soon, it's almost always destructive and ill-advised.

## 3. Review the personnel folders of each person who reports to you.

Look for strengths and positive factors that you can use to help the team succeed. Things that will tell you a lot about workers are:

- Training records. What courses, seminars and workshops has each employee attended? What courses at a local college or technical school has each employee taken?

- Attendance records. If the personnel department does not have them, you probably can get this from the payroll department.

- Sick-time usage. How often a person is sick may tell you a lot about his or her mental attitude and stress levels.

- Previous disciplinary records. Often these will tell you as much about the previous supervisor as the employees. If the person who held this position before you made mistakes, learn what you should avoid.

- Number of grievances filed and their nature. If you work in a union shop, you obviously have to abide by the union's contract, but be aware of employees who are grievance-prone. Try to build alliances to prevent trouble before it begins.

## 4. Identify the people who make things work.

Gain the support of these people as soon as possible. An effective way to do this is to review their past projects and note the contributions they've made. During your first meeting with them, tell them what you know about their accomplishments and the types of things you would like to continue.

## 5. Hold a meeting with all your staff.

Use this meeting to find out what the people who report to you want and need. Keep this meeting fairly informal. Use the following general outline during this meeting:

- Introduce yourself. If you've come from outside the department, briefly tell employees what you have been doing and where.

- Tell them what management expects from you.

- Tell them what your ideal vision is for the group. Be specific. Tell them what you care about—the good things and bad.

- Open a discussion. Ask them what they think the group needs to achieve this vision. Encourage them to talk about their concerns. Note the most important points on a flip chart. Treat these as action items and put dates on some of them to emphasize that you are action oriented.

- Summarize the key issues. Tell them you will be coming to them for help and more information about these issues.

- Thank them and close the meeting.

- Be sure you follow up and do the things you said you were going to do.

## 6. Ignore rumors and gossip.

This is especially important for destructive comments made by one worker about others. If you catch someone doing this, make it clear you will not tolerate it. Some people will tell you things to ingratiate themselves to you. This must stop immediately. If there are rumors floating around, find their source and quickly set the record straight.

## 7. Be upbeat and positive.

If the company is going through a difficult time, be honest about what's going on without joining in discussions about how terrible the situation is. Direct your comments toward solutions—things you and your group can do to make conditions better. Even if the company is on the brink of failure, whining and complaining won't keep it open. It may, in fact, help it fail faster.

## 8. Know what management wants from you.

Get a clear idea of what your superiors want from you and from the group you lead. Let your staff know what your supervisors expect from you. This makes it possible for everyone to establish priorities and understand why projects change. For instance, is the focus on:

- Numbers, productivity?
- Quality?
- Customer-service issues?
- Reducing overhead, reducing costs?

## 9. Set high goals for yourself and your group.

Communicate your goals to your team. Tell your staff members how they're doing against the standards you've communicated to them. Do everything you can to link each employee's responsibilities to these goals.

The key thing to remember is that you need the people who work for you to understand your vision. You are the chief salesperson of that vision, and it often has to be sold over and over again. Remember, you do *not* get paid for what you do, you get paid for what your staff does!

---

How would you handle the following situations?

- You were recently promoted to supervisor of the department in which you've worked for five years. You know your co-worker, Alyse, had hoped to get the position. She's a valuable worker and has many friends in the company. It would help if you could have her on your side. What will you do?

- It's your first day on the job as a supervisor for a new company. The only information you have about the people you supervise is in their personnel records. When the company hired you, you were told there were morale problems in this department. What do you do on your first day?

- Your new job is to supervise some highly technical people working in a field unfamiliar to you. The people are motivated and self-directed. Your primary duties will be to handle the budget and administrative details. What should your relationship be with your staff?

---

Take a few minutes to assess how the system at your workplace affects productivity. Circle the number you think most accurately reflects your company's way of doing business.

1. It's easy to get the tools and training my department needs.

   |     1     |     2     |     3     |     4     |     5     |
   |-----------|-----------|-----------|-----------|-----------|
   | Rarely    |           |           |           | Often     |

2. Other departments work well with my department. We often share ideas and resources with other departments.

   |     1     |     2     |     3     |     4     |     5     |
   |-----------|-----------|-----------|-----------|-----------|
   | Rarely    |           |           |           | Often     |

3. There's a feeling of teamwork at my company. All departments know that they're dependent upon all company employees for their success.

   |     1     |     2     |     3     |     4     |     5     |
   |-----------|-----------|-----------|-----------|-----------|
   | Rarely    |           |           |           | Often     |

4. Management doesn't play favorites. It recognizes the worth of all people who work there.

   |     1     |     2     |     3     |     4     |     5     |
   |-----------|-----------|-----------|-----------|-----------|
   | Rarely    |           |           |           | Often     |

## Your Turn

If you marked any of your answers a "1" or "2," you've identified some of the ways the system may be working against your staff. Think of some ways you can circumvent the problems. List them in the space below as well as some ways you can prevent the system from sabotaging the effectiveness of the people who work for you.

What is your vision of leadership? Fill in the columns below to help you gain a clear vision of where you want to go and what you want to achieve as a supervisor.

**Goals I want to achieve:**

_____     _____
_____     _____
_____     _____
_____     _____

**Contributions I want to make:**

_____     _____
_____     _____
_____     _____
_____     _____

**Things I want to help others to do:**

_____     _____
_____     _____
_____     _____
_____     _____

**Qualities I want to be remembered for:**

_____     _____
_____     _____
_____     _____
_____     _____

Circle three items in each section that are the most important to you. Then complete the following vision statement, using the items that you picked as most important to you.

---

**My Vision**

I want to achieve [write your goals] _____

_____

because I want to contribute more [write desired contributions] _____

_____

to the world and help others [write the things you want to help others achieve]_____

_____.

By doing this, I hope I will be remembered as a person who was [write the things you want to be remembered for]_____

_____

_____.

---

## Give Away Power to Gain Power

One of the hardest things for a supervisor is letting go of some of the responsibility for getting the job done to the very people who must do the work. Yet, as a leader, you must have confidence in your people to get the job done.

There is an unwritten rule about power that goes like this: *If you don't give power, you won't get power.*

Some supervisors say, "You can't leave people on their own. Nothing would ever get done." This is a fine example of self-fulfilling prophecy. When your company promoted you to a supervisory position, it gave you responsibility. You willingly met that responsibility. The same process works with those who work for you. Remember, if you can't give trust, you won't get trust in return.

It comes down to delegating tasks and releasing some of the power to others. Successful delegation is truly a win-win situation. It allows you to direct your attention toward larger and more pressing issues, and it allows your employees to grow and feel more pride in themselves.

There are four basic steps of successful delegation:

1. Assign the work to the appropriate team member.
2. Get the agreement and commitment of the worker to perform the duties well.
3. Give the person sufficient authority to do the job.
4. Set a time for the employee to report back to you. Don't double-check the individual's work every few minutes. Find out what went right and what difficulties there were. Help the employee to learn from that difficulty.

When you empower others by delegating, you open the door to an incredible storehouse of knowledge and experience. If you empower others, you all win and win big.

When you delegate, you must give enough authority to get the job done. Stand behind that person and his decisions. Make sure others know he has the authority. And if this is the first time this person has had this kind of responsibility, teach him how to use authority wisely.

You will not lose power or authority if you ask your people for their help. When you share responsibility, when you empower your people, you share in their glory when they succeed. The best praise a supervisor can receive is a compliment given to one of his team members. You grow when you get responsibility, and you grow when you give it. Be a good teacher. Help your employees develop, and achieve more of your personal goals than you ever thought possible by trusting others—and yourself—and delegating whenever possible.

What makes it hard for *you* to delegate? Take the following quiz to determine why delegating may be difficult for you.

**True  False**

| True | False | |
|------|-------|---|
| T | F | 1. It's easier to do it myself. It takes too long to explain something over and over again. |
| T | F | 2. The person I delegate a task to will get all of the credit, and management may think he or she is more qualified than I. |
| T | F | 3. I am afraid the person will botch the job. |
| T | F | 4. I fear my employees might think I'm making them do more work. |
| T | F | 5. I'm not sure that this is a task that can be delegated. |
| T | F | 6. My boss may disapprove of me delegating a task that she assigned me to do. |

**Interpretation**

1. If you answered "true," stop and think about whether it's more important to get the job done exactly as you would do it or to help others learn to do the job. Think about how much patience you have and whether you're willing to share your knowledge with others.

2. If you answered "true," examine your self-esteem. Do you secretly feel you don't deserve to be a supervisor? Remember, management already has faith in your abilities. Work on having faith in yourself, too.

3. If you answered "true," consider what's the worst thing that can happen. What safeguards can you build into the job to feel better about delegating?

4. If you answered "true," remember that your trust in someone's ability to do the job is the greatest compliment you can give him. When the people on your staff get recognition and support from you, they welcome an opportunity to shine.

5. If you answered "true," remember that common sense goes a long way here. If it doesn't involve privileged information or setting policies, then it probably can be delegated.

6. If you answered "true," you may be surprised that your boss wants you to delegate more. She wants you to use the people who report to you to get the job done—not to do everything yourself.

## Summary

A supervisor is many things. Most importantly, a good supervisor is someone who:

- Doesn't lose his temper when things go wrong.
- Gets things done.
- Can admit mistakes and move on.
- Is clear about what she wants from others.
- Always knows what's going on.
- Is upbeat and positive.
- Has vision.
- Gives praise freely and specifically.
- Is organized.
- Protects his staff from interference.
- Lets the staff members know how they are doing.
- Sets a good personal example.
- Involves others in the decision-making process.
- Regularly praises and rewards the people who report to her.
- Enforces the rules fairly.
- Doesn't complain and gets on with the job.
- Never plays favorites.
- Can delegate authority and tasks to others.
- Presents a neat, clean appearance.
- Doesn't talk "down to" or "up to" anyone.
- Has courage.
- Supports supervisors and never makes negative comments about those she works for.
- Doesn't misuse authority.
- Makes sure his staff members are well-trained in their jobs.
- Communicates, communicates and communicates.
- Doesn't shirk responsibility or pass the blame to others.
- Avoids generalities when assigning tasks; is goal-oriented and specific.

# Chapter 2

# Goals, Purposes and Targets

## What you'll learn:

- How to set meaningful goals and develop plans to achieve them.

- How to use value-added thinking to guide your decisions.

- How to reduce complexity and increase your job satisfaction.

As a supervisor, it's your job to determine the exact goal, purpose and/or desired activity of the department you lead and every project you do. If you're going to lead, you must know where you're going.

## What Is Your Product?

Before you can set goals, you must know precisely what your department is expected to produce. Products are either physical objects or services. Whichever they are, there are important quality distinctions that must be made. A good product is a completed thing that meets all quality standards. Products that are flawed are incomplete. Therefore, they're not real products. Here are some examples of good products:

- A well-written report, free of errors.
- An automobile door that fits excellently and functions to specifications.
- A cup of coffee that meets all the requirements of taste, price, quality and timely delivery.
- Mail delivered on time and undamaged.
- A meal properly cooked and delivered.

If your staff members don't have a good grasp of what their products are, don't be surprised if they make mistakes or waste energy doing the wrong things.

As a supervisor, you're in contact with numbers every day. You have to deal with schedules, production numbers, quality measures, costs and research data. It seems endless. That's the nature of business. However, when numbers become the guiding principles in a department or company, there can be consequences, often quite severe.

If you specify that numbers are important, workers will give you what you want. Setting targets based on numbers alone is a bad idea and may be very unproductive in both the short and long run.

Your true objectives are subject to the demands of the marketplace, which increasingly is driven by factors other than numbers, including the following:

- How your markets are changing and evolving.
- Product quality.
- Ease of use.
- Accessibility.
- New marketing technologies.
- Competitive pricing.
- Time to market new products.
- People skills and training.

Consider the following examples in which numbers are the only target. Attempt to answer all of the questions.

1. Your department makes blue gadgets. You tell one worker her quota is 100 blue gadgets per day. However, the production line is capable of making only 80 blue gadgets per day. How many blue gadgets will the worker make?

    *If you said 80, you would be wrong. The worker will make 100. That's what you told her to make. The quality of the products will be poor and require rework, or there may be excessive scrap. However, the worker will produce 100 blue gadgets, maybe even 101, so she'll look good to her supervisor.*

2. Now let's say the production line is capable of producing 150 blue gadgets per day, but again you've told her the quota is 100. How many will she make?

    *You got it, 100; maybe 101 in order to look good for her supervisor.*

3. Now, imagine that the production line is capable of making 125 blue gadgets per day. What would you tell her is the quota? How would you inspire this employee to give 110 percent?

Modern customers make intelligent buying decisions. They're more discerning and have more choices than ever before. Additionally, they have access to better technology, which gives them more power over the selection process. Even more than establishing quantitative goals, it's important to have a mission—a reason for your department's product that goes beyond the marketplace. Your mission must reflect changes in the marketplace, your customer's expectations and your staff's desire to provide a product that has meaning. When you set goals for your people, you must consider all of these factors. Furthermore, your department's goals and mission must have meaning for your employees.

To create a meaningful mission for your department, ask yourself the following questions:

1. What is your department's product? What does your department exchange with other departments or provide for the customer? Does your staff know what the products are?

2. Have you included a statement about quality in your mission? How does customer service fit into your mission? Does the department's mission include the enhancement of its people? Do your numbers measure things besides productivity?

3. Do you view your department as both a customer and a supplier? Do you know who your internal customers are? Do you know who your internal suppliers are? Do you know what quality products your customers want from you and your people? Have you created methods to measure how well you and your people are meeting customer needs?

4. Have you involved all the members of your department in creating the mission? Have you created a mission or vision statement for your group? Have you involved your people in defining the department's objectives and written them down in simple declarative sentences?

Have you regularly reviewed departmental goals and objectives with your staff? Have you developed measurable ways to show your staff how well they are doing? Do the people who report to you understand how their jobs add value to the company's products?

To have meaning, your mission and your principles must be aligned. Answer the following questions to determine the principles that guide your mission.

1. What is more important—being honest or being the best?

2. Is it more important to enjoy your job or to get the job done, no matter what it takes?

3. What do you consider a satisfying day at work—everyone working together as a team or meeting a difficult deadline?

4. Do you think people have to believe their company's product or service is the best in order to excel, or do you think people find personal satisfaction in their own abilities?

5. Which statement do you agree with most?
   a. Everyone should get along on the job and work together.
   b. A little competition among co-workers can be fun.

Your answers to these questions should help you determine more about your personal principles. If you selected the first choice in the majority of the questions, you're a "people person" and would do well to incorporate some principles about teamwork in your mission statement. And if you selected the second choice in the majority of the questions, you're more project-oriented. Under your leadership, people can find new depths of ability, as long as they understand their goals through your mission statement.

## What Makes a Plan Work?

Great plans stand on perfect attention to detail. However, plans also have a way of changing, thus erasing all your careful attention to detail. To create a plan that will succeed, be sure to include the following:

- **A well-defined objective.** "I would like to own a new Ferrari" is a dream, not an objective. To own a new Ferrari before the year 2010 is a valid objective.

- **Clearly defined steps.** These are the steps that will help you achieve the objective. A wish list doesn't get the job done.

- **Resources required.** Assign the correct resources (people, money, materials) for each step.

- **A team to do the job.** You want people who have the skills and determination to accomplish your team's task. The ability to assemble an effective team may be the most important skill a supervisor has.

- **A realistic timeline.** Make this tough enough to get the adrenaline flowing, but not so tough the team can't meet it.

- **A method to measure your effectiveness.** It's important to develop measurements that are more than "wallpaper charts."

## Planning and Continuous Improvement

Dr. W. Edwards Deming created the Shewhart Cycle to illustrate how to plan for continuous, never-ending improvement. Deming named the chart after his teacher, the man who pioneered statistical process control in the 1920s. It's also called the PDCA Cycle—Plan, Do, Check, Act Cycle. (See Figure 2.1 on page 33.) The PDCA cycle has four phases:

- *Plan:* A company or department plans a project or improvement.
- *Do:* Then people do the project or activity.
- *Check:* They analyze the results.
- *Act:* Then they act either to standardize the change or begin the cycle of improvement again with new information.

## The PDCA Cycle

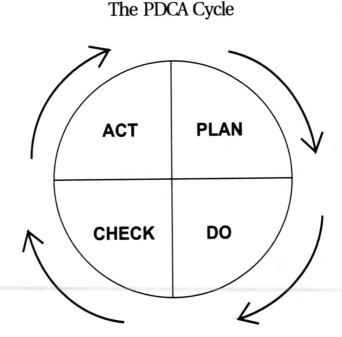

*Figure 2.1. The Shewhart Cycle: Plan-Do-Check-Act*

The PDCA approach is a tool to help a supervisor think inclusively when planning projects and activities. It helps you look at work as a continuous process to be evaluated and assessed and then modified to encourage even greater efficiency and quality.

There are dozens of planning tools available to supervisors: books, pre-designed charts, software, etc. Become familiar with what's available and stay current with new methods and techniques.

Regardless of the tools you use, the basic elements of a plan are the same, whether you're updating equipment or developing a new advertising campaign. Include the following in your plan and you won't go wrong.

- Mission, goals and objectives.
- Methods to achieve goals and objectives.
- Timeline.
- Assignment of personnel.
- Determination and management of costs.
- Tests for effectiveness.
- Corrections of performance using the data you have gathered.
- Adjustment of the plan.
- A repeat of the above.

Use this list to form questions about your plan and check its completeness. Spend that extra hour or two developing your plan. It can save you days, even weeks, later on.

## The Supervisor's Role as a Decision-Maker

Making decisions is an important part of a supervisor's job. Whenever you make a decision, you must choose between two or more courses of action. You may have heard you should first get the facts when making a decision. However, just as important is determining the relevance of the information used in decision-making. Or, as Dr. Perry Gluckman says:

*Until you have data as a backup,*
*you're just another person with an opinion.*

You must first sift the data for relevance and test opinions against reality. You must have the right yardstick to measure the facts.

As the courses of action that can be taken are discussed and evaluated, boundaries quickly become apparent. If you take one course of action, certain limitations will have to be considered. If you take another course of action, other limitations must be taken into consideration.

These boundaries are valuable in helping you decide what facts still need to be gathered so you can make a decision. Often, these boundaries reveal the answers you need for making the best decision at the time.

For example, if Joe, your lead machinist, says the turret lathe is a piece of junk and suggests scrapping it for a newer model, you must first determine what the relevant facts are. Is the statement that the equipment is "a piece of junk" relevant? Maybe. But then you look at what is being produced by that machine. New lathes are expensive. So you ask the question, "Do the products made on this machine justify its replacement?" What are the cost/earnings numbers for the machine? What boundaries should be taken into consideration when deciding whether to replace the lathe?

It's important to look closely at the issue at hand while never losing sight of the big picture. For instance, your staff may want training in a new technology, but your company isn't implementing that technology for a year or more. The training, therefore, wouldn't add value if provided too soon.

To find out if you're making the best decision you can make at the time, ask yourself the following questions and write your answers in the blank spaces.

1. Are there any subject matter experts whom I can go to for information?

*If you're having trouble making a decision, it's likely you don't feel confident about your information. Look for advice from others who have studied the problem you face.*

2. Who are the people close to the problem? Have I asked them for their ideas?

*Often, the best ideas for resolving a problem come from the people who work the closest to it. They're just waiting for someone to ask!*

3. Am I trying to make a decision too quickly? If so, why?

*"Haste makes waste" has more than a little ring of truth. Don't allow others or yourself to pressure you to make quick decisions.*

4. Have I applied financial tools to the problem, from the standpoint of both the short-term and the long-term?

*The bottom line often holds the answer to making a decision. Whenever you need to make a decision, do the figures and see how much your decision will cost both in the immediate future and down the road.*

Considering the "value-addedness" of your decisions is critical in today's business world. This viewpoint teaches you to look at the value-added at all levels of business operation, from the simplest process to the structure of an entire department, through a whole line of products. Because it focuses on the value of the end product, a value-added viewpoint can help you make better decisions more quickly.

Thinking in terms of added value is helpful when deciding if individuals, teams and even departments are operating as they should.

There are many tools available to determine the value of business processes. For example, a tool called Activity-Based Costing (ABC) allows a supervisor to gather costs, define cost drivers and cost centers, etc. Cost of Quality, a technique developed by Phillip B. Crosby, gives a supervisor a tool to determine how quality is really affecting the bottom line. Statistical Process Control (SPC) is a technique that uses basic statistics to measure the variation in manufacturing and business processes. If these are mentioned, they should be explained in greater detail or through examples.

Think of it in terms of dollars, if you like. Your company's chief financial officer does. Iron ore dug from a mine in Minnesota sells for so much a ton. The railroad company charges so much per ton to ship it to the smelter. Add that to the cost of the ore. The smelting company charges so much per ton for each iron ingot. Add this to the previous two steps. The steel forming and shaping plant charges so much per ton for processed steel products, which in turn are purchased by the machinery manufacturer. The machinery manufacturer adds value to the sheet and bar stock and makes products that are sold to other factories.

Anything along this line that affects value, reduces the cost/benefit margin or affects the profit of the company involved in that step must be watched closely. Add to this the demands of competition and the market, and you have the key to one company's success and another's failure.

On the other hand, there are things that don't add value, such as:

- Incorrect pricing
- Targeting the wrong market
- Endless meetings during which nothing of importance is accomplished
- Shipping errors
- Late deliveries
- Defective goods
- Scrap and rework
- Design flaws
- Poorly maintained equipment
- Insufficient training of personnel
- Legal difficulties

You have probably seen most of these. It's imperative that every supervisor knows how to add value and eliminate everything that doesn't. You must think and act as if it's your budget, your checkbook and your job that's on the line, because it is!

## Value-Added Thinking in Your Department

When you face your daily tasks and try to decide what has priority, ask yourself: "Does this activity add value to products I am responsible for producing?" Then ask, "What should I do to get value-added thinking from my people?"

Ask yourself the following questions to determine if you're doing all you can to be certain everyone in your department understands their roles in the "big picture."

1. Do you keep your employees informed about corporate decisions you learn about in management meetings?

2. Have you identified departments that are your department's "customers" and made a point to understand what they need from you?

3. Do you encourage your staff to share resources and ideas with other departments?

4. If there's a conflict with another department, do you attempt to resolve it by communicating and compromising?

5. Are you proactive in identifying potential conflicts and informing your staff about changes that may need to be made?

6. Do you "lobby" for your department by attending meetings and educating others within the company about what your department can and can't do?

7. Do you assign interdepartmental projects to your staff members and give them time to be on committees that affect corporate direction?

The best answer lies in showing employees how and where their roles in the operation add value to the company's products. Show the "upstream" and "downstream" effects of each operation, how delays and errors have far-reaching effects. The "stone that causes ripples in the pool" is an effective analogy. Get your employees to see their actions as waves radiating outward, eventually to the customer—and to their own paychecks.

There are hundreds of ways for you to bring this attitude into play every day. Put a large sign over your desk that says, "Am I adding value to processes, products and services?" If your answer is "yes," then you're winning on the job.

## Complexity vs. Simplicity

One simple, important way you can add value in your department is to eliminate unnecessary complexity. When one of your staff tells you that she knows a way to make something less complex or complicated, listen. She's probably going to save you time and money!

Many people see a task as complex and difficult to accomplish. However, if you analyze how these people perform tasks, you'll usually see that they add unnecessary complexity to their jobs by doing things such as:

- Unnecessary steps

- Errors, inside and outside the department

- Rework: doing over what should have been done right the first time

- Duplication of effort

- Unnecessary delays

- "Fire-fighting "

If you examine the tasks performed by your staff members, you'll find some caused by errors introduced into the system. Often people won't even recognize the errors. If you ask someone, "Why are you doing that?" he'll likely answer, "Because we've always done it this way."

Figure 2.2 illustrates the amount of complexity found in most companies. The figure's segments are self-explanatory except perhaps "Time Unavailable for Work." This includes things like meals, breaks, holidays, sick time, etc. As supervisor, you determine when and where your staff wastes time and money.

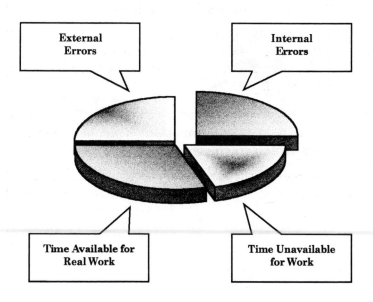

*Figure 2.2. Time Lost Due to External and Internal Errors*

Following are some typical examples of added complexity.

- A person who opens and restocks customer returns. If the order is filled correctly or meets the customer's expectations in the first place, much of this may not be necessary.

- Customer service representatives who must repeatedly call late-paying customers because the billing system is inadequate.

- Having to hire a person to expedite late and missing orders because the people responsible for filling orders aren't held accountable.

- Hiring an inspector to look for defects. A simpler process, used at numerous world-class manufacturing companies, is to train the workers to be their own inspectors.

- Meetings that don't support your objectives.

- Having to ask for explanations of written reports or having to verify reports you're given.

List some of the unnecessary added complexities that occur in your department and throughout your company.

_____

_____

_____

_____

You know there's too much complexity when everything seems to be a crisis that requires immediate attention.

# What You Can Do to Reduce Complexity

The following seven activities can significantly reduce the complexity in your department or group.

## 1. Do a "productive work vs. non-productive work" survey.

In addition to doing this yourself, ask each person on your staff to record the following data for two weeks.

- List tasks that truly contribute to the products they're supposed to produce.

- List all the tasks that subtract from the time needed to complete products.

- Log the time spent on both activities, productive and non-productive.

## 2. Develop flowcharts.

Have your staff members chart all the steps in their processes, not as you want them to be, but as they are actually performed now. List even the wasted steps. If employees have more than one job, have them do flowcharts on each one separately. (See flowcharts on the next page.)

After they've created their flowcharts and assigned timelines for getting their jobs done, review each process with each employee and ask the following questions:

- Is this really where the process starts? Is there anything you should do or need to have earlier?

- At each point, ask, "Does it always happen this way? Does anything go wrong here?"

- Modify the chart according to the answers to these questions and have your employees redo the flowchart as they should be. You want copies of both "as is" and "to be" flowcharts.

During the flowchart process, you will discover opportunities to save the company quite a lot of money and time. You'll see areas where you can make simple, on-the-spot fixes. This exercise often reveals whether the right people are doing the right jobs and helps you gain a better understanding of what your people face every day.

As an added benefit, the flowcharts will provide valuable documentation that can easily be the basis of written work instructions and training materials for new staff members. Another important benefit is that this exercise gives everyone on your staff a sense of belonging to a team.

Remember, when employees tell you something is too complex, be polite, but then go show them how to make it simpler. Every time you change something complex into something simple, you save the company money. And don't forget to reward your staff members when they simplify a complex task.

### 3. Delegate authority and tasks.

Unload tasks that eat up your time and that others can do as well as you.

### 4. Prioritize your activities.

If there's one thing to learn from the lives of great executives, it's how they concentrate their efforts. Effective supervisors do first things first, and they do them one step at a time.

### 5. Complete what you start.

The basic life cycle of anything in the universe is birth, change, decline and death. Or think of it as start, change, stop. All things, great and small, follow the same sequence. However, people often become stuck in one part of the cycle. Some people are great at starting things, but aren't so great at changing and stopping. Others do best at changing things. A few others are good at trying to stop things, even before an activity has started or changed.

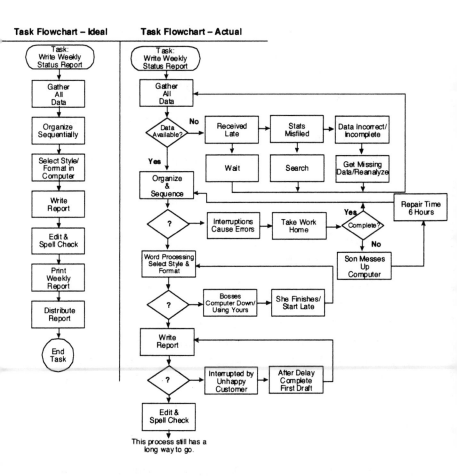

*Figure 2.3. Sample Flowchart Comparing
Ideal vs. Actual Task Flow*

## 6. Get people to put things in writing.

When there are a lot of verbal orders, instructions or suggestions floating around, complexity increases. There's nothing wrong with figuring things out on the spot; however, as the saying goes, "There are many slips between the cup and the lip."

Putting things in writing doesn't mean you stop talking to people. You just need to establish procedures for getting certain communications in writing. Here are some of them:

- Any event affecting the production schedule.

- Input from other departments involving changes to product specifications.

- Input from customers affecting the design, delivery or cost of products.

- Expenditure requests from subordinates. (Use your judgment and allow certain workers to purchase supplies up to a certain limit.)

- Requests for time off.

- Suggestions for improvements, upgrades and ways to save time or money.

- All formal activities such as staff meetings, policy updates, change control meetings, etc. (Calling people at the last minute and telling them there is a meeting is disruptive and unproductive.)

## 7. Take notes.

Another way to reduce complexity is to write notes to remind yourself of things you need to do. Whenever you talk with members of your staff or co-workers in other departments, take notes on important discussions and file them for future reference.

Forgetting to handle problems your staff tells you about or forgetting to tell employees you're working on them is the sign of a poor supervisor. Your people will quickly lose confidence in you and lose their desire to do well on the job.

Your employees don't expect you to be a memory machine, but they do expect you to follow up on problems they told you about, especially ones you've said you would take care of. Workers don't forgive a supervisor who doesn't keep her word, and when people don't keep their word business doesn't prosper.

Include in your notes anything that can affect schedules or how you plan your time. Write down when and where things happened, where you were when you received certain information, the name of the person you talked with, what was said and what happened.

---

Good internal communication should include the following information:

1. Date and Time. (Optional: You might want to send out additional reminder notices.)

2. Place.

3. Form. (How the event, whatever it is, will occur. Is there a sequence of events? Are data or materials required?)

4. Event/Subject. (Is this a policy document, a call for a departmental meeting, etc.?)

Most of all, be specific! Good communications reduce errors and serve notice that you place importance on controlling your time and your directions.

---

# Summary

- A supervisor is responsible for determining the goals of the department and how they relate to a meaningful mission.

- To truly motivate your employees to do their best, your department's mission must be related to more than numbers.

- Before you can set goals, you must know precisely what your department is expected to produce, keeping in mind that anything your staff produces that's flawed isn't a real product.

- One of the keys to developing meaningful goals is to adopt a value-added viewpoint—looking at the value added by each process carried out in your department.

- You add value when you eliminate unnecessary complexity that affects the bottom line.

# Chapter 3

# Managing Time and Stress

## What you'll learn:

- How to better control your time.
- How to handle stress.
- How to recognize signs of trouble in your department.

The limiting factor in any process is the scarcest resource. When you're a supervisor, time is often the resource that most limits how much you can accomplish.

Time is a quantity much like a bank balance. You must watch it and use it carefully. If you don't, you probably will find yourself burning the midnight oil, trying to get back that which has been irretrievably lost. It isn't the tasks you have to accomplish that break your back, it's the amount of time in which you have to do them.

There are three key things you must do to best utilize and control your time.

1. Measure it: Keep a calendar so you know what's supposed to happen on any given day. Also keep a log, so you know exactly how you're really spending your time.

2. Manage it: Set priorities. Decide when to do certain tasks and determine what tasks to delegate to others.

3. Accumulate it: Set aside enough time to accomplish major tasks.

More and more, managers are taking work home that requires large blocks of their time. It's the only place where the phone doesn't ring nonstop, the boss doesn't want to talk about his golf game and employees don't need help with their problems.

Taking work home, however, has many hidden costs. These costs hide in the evenings and weekends you're too busy to enjoy your family. Furthermore, the point will come when even taking work home won't get the job done. You run into the law of diminishing returns. Time can't expand. You can't stretch it without something snapping.

And you can't determine the most efficient way to use your time if you don't know how and on what your time is spent from week to week. It's critical to make a list of the most important things you know you have to do every day for a week or month and compare it to your record of what you actually do. How closely do they match?

A simple activities/work log is a good time management tool. Use this log to keep track of your work activities for several weeks. Continue doing this long enough to include a representative sample of all the activities you're likely to encounter in your position as a supervisor. List each task you do during the day and how much time you spend on it. For instance, if you're delayed in finishing a task because of missing data or a malfunctioning computer, record this. Sort out activities that are really productive from those that aren't.

# Take Control of Your Time

As you rise within your organization, the demands on your time will increase. You need larger blocks of time. You can't write an effective report in 10-minute increments over the next several weeks. You can't facilitate problem-solving teams by meeting 15 minutes once every week. The report could take 10 hours to complete, even for the first draft. Problem-solving teams typically meet for one to two hours at a time. It also takes concentration to sit down and plan the activities, products and goals you want from your staff. And if you spend too little time with your employees on an individual basis, they may feel slighted or charge off in the wrong direction.

But what can you do, for example, if your boss wants to talk about his son's last soccer game when you have several pressing tasks to do? Or when one of your people has a birthday party you must attend?

There's no such thing as a perfect world, but if you do any or all of the following, you'll make tremendous progress toward controlling how and where your time is spent.

- Use the work log to find out exactly where your time is going now.

- Delegate as many tasks as possible. A good rule of thumb is if a job or task is done more than once, delegate it!

- Take advantage of new technology like electronic calendars, faxes, video-conferencing, the Internet, teleconferencing and voice mail. Consider it a good investment for you and your company to attend seminars on these new technologies.

- Whenever possible, make decisions yourself rather than by committee.

- Don't put off unpleasant tasks.

- Encourage people to make appointments when they want to see you rather than allowing them to stop by unannounced.

- When you hold a meeting, establish a clear, concise agenda and send it out well in advance. Allow only the items on the agenda to be discussed.

- Arrange your day to take advantage of your own energy and creative strength. For example, do not make decisions when you're tired or ill. You will probably end up having to make them again.

- Encourage your staff to be problem-solvers and make decisions on their own. When they make mistakes, don't get angry. Help them figure out how to avoid making the same mistake again.

- Set aside a quiet time every day to review past, present and future events so you can learn, plan and create.

- Whenever possible, complete tasks at one sitting. Real energy is gained from completing things. It's better not to start a project at all than to get a quarter of the way through it and then leave with your attention stuck on an incompleted task.

- Handle each piece of paper only once. Make a decision on what to do with it when you get it.

- Make efficient use of "wait time." Read and catch up on correspondence while you're waiting for someone to call you or for a meeting to begin.

Successful supervisors are successful managers of time. If you have a secretary or assistant, make sure this person knows your number-one need is to have more time to focus on high-priority tasks. Any efforts you make to acquire more time will pay off in the short and long run.

# How You Can Get Larger Blocks of Time

One very effective way to get more time is to teach your staff to work, plan and make decisions independently. Also, as much as possible, get the information you need electronically or on paper using e-mail, faxes or written reports. It's much faster to read something than have it explained to you verbally.

Above all, don't make important decisions hastily. If you're wrong, you will have to make corrections, which generally takes a great deal more time than doing it right in the first place. If you take a little more time to plan your daily tasks, you'll save yourself large quantities of precious time downstream.

Arrange your day so you can handle all correspondence, e-mail, telephone calls, etc. during a block of time when you won't be interrupted.

Don't take a Band-Aid approach to time management. We are talking about a top-level process here. If you want more time for the important things, you have to make big changes. It's to your advantage to put as much thought and care into time management as a decision to change the work flow of your entire department.

If you've just come from another management position, be sure someone can replace you in your old post. Otherwise, you'll never totally get rid of the old position. People will call you every 20 minutes with problems. Remember, your new job needs and deserves all of your attention.

Bottom line: Let go. There's a tendency for those who have come up through the "trenches" to want to keep track of every detail because that's what makes them the most comfortable. Don't fall prey to this. You don't have time. That's someone else's job now.

To manage your time more effectively, look at the things that waste your time *and* the things you do to contribute to the problem. Circle the letter that most closely matches how you would react.

1. Your boss at your previous job calls you at your new office to complain about his job. You:
   a. Engage in a lengthy conversation, even though you have deadlines to meet. It's nice to be treated as an equal.
   b. Tell your old boss you'd love to talk, but you're busy now and suggest having lunch together.

2. Your boss keeps giving you more work, and now you can't seem to get anything done because she keeps switching priorities. You:
   a. Suffer in silence and do the best you can.
   b. Tell your boss what you can and can't do and ask her to write the priorities down so you can both remember and refer to them.

3. One of your staff comes to your office, wanting to talk about a personal problem. You have a meeting in one-half hour. You:
   a. Grit your teeth and listen.
   b. Acknowledge his emotional state and tell him that you can talk later.

Here's what your responses mean:

1. If you answered "a," examine why it's more important to you to discuss your old job than get on with your new one. Having lunch (b) is a fairer option for both you and the company for which you now work.

2. Saying "no" is an important part of time management—even if you have to say "no" to your boss! Answering "b" will help you get a handle on your time much faster than suffering in silence.

3. You can't always be available to solve other people's problems. When employees are emotional, giving them some time alone is often a better option than taking up your time talking with them.

# How to Control and Reduce Stress

In addition to trying to control your time, you'll probably stand in the middle of a hurricane of activity every day. This whirlwind contains projects, people, electronic elements, communications, and ideas—all in almost continual motion and threatening to overwhelm you by their sheer numbers. Is it any wonder that you often feel stressed out?

To take control of stress, you must first understand what causes it. In any stressful situation, there are two components you must deal with: the cause of the stress and its effect on you.

For example, if the IRS sends you a threatening letter that suggests a horde of agents is about to descend on you, you're probably going to feel stressed. The letter is the cause, and your feelings are the "effect" of that letter. Because you don't have all the data you need to deal with the letter yet, you're affected by stress.

Let's say that you call the IRS and learn that the letter was sent to you by mistake. The anxiety is gone; the stress is gone. Calling the IRS and learning the truth caused your anxiety to go away. The effect was the relief of stress.

In your daily life, you'll find that you can reduce a lot of stress by handling one thing at a time. Make a decision and then work at it until it's finished or you've done as much as you can at that moment. If someone tries to get you started on something else, say no! When you've completed a task, move on to the next. Just remember, one thing at a time.

When you're feeling stressed, stop and ask yourself if any of the following things are happening to you.

- Is something threatening my beliefs, values, security or well-being?
- Am I trying to adjust to rapid change?

- Have I lost control of something and, therefore, feel vulnerable?

- Have my expectations not been realized?

When you determine what's truly causing your stress, take steps to alleviate the problem. Even if you can't resolve the situation immediately, taking control often relieves a great deal of the stress you're feeling.

Resisting and avoiding stress are two surefire stress-producers or, at the very least, they'll maintain a stressful condition. By confronting and adapting to stress, however, you move away from it toward better mental and physical health.

## Handling Stress of a Troubled Department

Trouble at work is a stress-producer, especially if you're in charge of a troubled department. You feel you should have your finger on the pulse of the situation, but trouble appears before you even realize there's a problem.

When trouble exists in a department, it's often possible to turn it around before things get ugly—if you catch it early enough. How can you determine when things aren't going well before the whole place goes up in flames?

When things are going wrong in a department or even the whole company, there are warning signs. Review the following list often. Ask yourself, "Do these conditions exist here?"

- People operate in a state of fear. They're afraid to speak up. They are especially fearful about speaking up in front of management

- The company has several small cliques that don't trust each other.

- No one is getting or giving training.

There are three typical responses to stress: resistance, avoidance or confrontation. Circle the letter indicating your normal response to the following situations:

1. It's been one of those days. The computer system went down, your boss yelled at you, and traffic was a nightmare. You:

   a. Fight back by getting angry.
   b. Pretend you don't feel pressured.
   c. Adapt to the situation by recognizing that while on some days it doesn't pay to get out of bed, tomorrow will surely be better.

2. You were thrilled to be named the leader of the new project team, but now it seems that you can't get anything done. Everyone is coming at you, needing something. It's driving you crazy! You:

   a. Yell at everyone to leave you alone.
   b. Shut your door and forward your phone to voice mail.
   c. Develop a different way for people to communicate their needs to you (preferably in written form).

3. You've been given a job you're not sure you can do. You're afraid you would lose face if you told your boss about your concerns, but there is a great deal riding on this—both for you and your company. You:

   a. Plunge ahead and hope for the best.
   b. Put off the work.
   c. Tell your boss your fears and ask for help.

- People talk about each other rather than problems with their jobs.

- Work areas are sloppy, dirty, and disorderly. Machines, tools, and materials are not properly stocked or well-maintained.

- Absenteeism, sick time, and unaccounted absences are unusually high.

- Scrap and rework numbers are unusually high.

- No promotions are being given.

- Communications are guarded or not taking place except under duress.

- Good people are leaving the company to find work elsewhere.

If you detect any of these signs, call your people together. Remember that any situation can be improved with real communication. The agenda for this meeting is quite simple. There are two basic questions to ask:

1. What's wrong with the department, team or group?
2. What can we do to fix the problems?

If several warning signs are present, be prepared for fireworks. This is where your patience, good will and determination pay off. To prevent potential problems, establish three basic ground rules for the meeting.

1. Set a goal for the meeting. For example, if rumors and half-truths are causing a problem, get the department back on track by stopping them or by finding out what's hurting the group and doing something about it. If you're having a problem identifying the goal, ask your employees to help.

2. Listen to everything people have to say, except personal attacks. If these problems exist, address them privately with the individuals involved.

3. Don't settle for half-answers or generalities. If you don't get a clear answer to the question, "What's wrong with our group?" ask it again in a different way and keep asking until you get an answer that makes sense to you.

As the meeting progresses, write down the major points on a flipchart. Don't dispute or disagree with anything your employees say. Acknowledge their input thoroughly and move on. When you ask someone to communicate with you, don't complain if you don't like the answers.

If people want to shout and get angry, let them, but don't join in. You're the referee. You have to keep people talking so you can get to the bottom of the problem.

After your group has thoroughly discussed what's wrong, find out what the entire group and the individuals in it can do to handle the problems. Take each item listed on the flipchart and ask, "What part of this problem can we do something about?" Of course, there are some problems you don't have the power to fix. Even if you can fix only part of a problem, it's a start in the right direction.

Never allow hopelessness to set in and never close a meeting on a note of futility. Assign tasks to people. Assign yourself tasks. Make everyone feel they can be a part of the solution.

Finally, agree to meet again and assess everyone's progress. Work with the situation as long as necessary or until you have enough momentum to put problem-solving in the hands of individuals and smaller groups.

## Handling Stress of Change

Change is another major stressor in the workplace, even if the change will make things better.

You can compare the process of change to a heart transplant. The body, like any organization, has strict operational rules. It has built-in methods of doing things and fights to maintain the status quo. There are mechanisms in the body that have been in place for a very long time. Moreover, this machinery has developed ways to protect itself against "foreign invasion"—change.

When the old heart fails and the new one is installed in the body, the body's protective mechanisms don't recognize this new heart as a good thing. Instead, the body perceives the new heart as a threat. The body attempts to reject and destroy it. Doctors—agents of change—introduce certain chemicals and medicines to overcome the body's old survival instructions. In this way, the new heart becomes a natural part of the body and aids in its continued survival. Even so, the body requires extraordinary care during and after the operation if it is going to live for any period of time.

Supervisors are also agents of change. When your company makes changes, your employees' protective mechanisms often won't allow them to see these as good things. It is up to you to provide the "medicine" and care while people "heal" from the changes being made.

To continue the parallel, think of the situation in these two ways:

1. The doctor gives the patient aspirin to reduce fever and control pain. The supervisor communicates all the parameters of a coming change to prevent pain and upset.

2. The doctor gives the patient digitalis to stimulate and regulate the heart. The supervisor gives employees as much control as possible to stimulate them to accept the change and to regulate the orderly implementation of change.

Whenever there's change, some people will do very well and require little care, while others won't survive at all. In either case, it's not a good idea for supervisors to take survival for granted during periods of change.

# Anticipating Change

Change is a fact of life in today's business world. As discussed earlier, it's up to the supervisor to provide stability during times of change. By recognizing areas where change is most likely to occur, you can ease the stress of change for both you and your staff. If you remain alert to the following, change won't take you by surprise.

## "High tech" vs. "low tech"

All through history, people have gone from being afraid of new technology to taking it for granted. What is "high tech" today is sure to be "low tech" tomorrow. For example, a few decades ago people said things like, "If people were meant to fly, God would have given them wings." Today, you're more likely to hear someone say, "I'll take the next flight to San Jose and see you late this afternoon."

Remember, the fingers became the abacus, which became the slide rule, which became the huge IBM mainframe computer, which became the desktop PC, which will become...who knows, something fearful to some and exciting to others! When confronting change, just be sure to communicate the opportunities that change presents to your team members.

Here are some questions you must ask upper management when changes are being made.

1. What kinds of change can we expect (personnel, technology, relocation, pay, etc.)?

2. Is there a timeline for what's coming?

3. What can my team and I do to make the change more acceptable? What can we do to help or even prevent it, if necessary?

4. What sacrifices will my people have to make?

5. Exactly who will be affected by the changes?

Once you get the answers, you must decide the best way to communicate the change to your staff, especially if it will have negative consequences for your department. Answer the following questions to determine how you'll help them deal with change.

1. Upper management says the change will require terminating at least two of the people on your staff. How can you tell them what is going on and prevent rumors?

2. The change proposal may eliminate your entire department. Although plans call for relocating each employee, many people will probably be upset. What do you tell them?

3. The change will require learning new technologies. Many of the people on your staff have been with the company for a long time, and you know they'll resist the change. How can you make the change seem more palatable to them?

## Change is normal

To survive, your company has to make changes. If you can't run away from it, ignore it, hide from it or attack it—which are all common reactions to change—you must come to grips with it. The supervisor must do even more. You must be the champion of change, a counselor to those having difficulty dealing with it, a judge of its effects and an interpreter of its future.

The number-one priority when implementing change is communication. When you see change on the horizon, find out the facts, determine where it's coming from, who's going to be affected and how, and communicate that to your people. However, don't just leave it at that. Find ways to give them as much control over change as possible.

# Lessen Stress of Change by Communicating

When your company anticipates a major change, don't attempt to shield employees from the truth. Be willing to talk dollars and cents. Don't assume your employees can't understand basic economics. After all, most of the people on your staff probably run households. They know, for instance, that if the company isn't making enough money on a particular product, changes will have to be made.

Here are some suggestions to help people accept change more readily.

- Translate problems into opportunities. Tell them the truth and find ways to make real challenges out of coming events.

- Tell your people what's going to happen and when. This comes under the heading of prediction and consequences. Allowing employees to find out only a week before a layoff occurs is cruel and unnecessary. Give people a chance to prepare for change.

- Have your employees become part of the company's new processes. Every step that gives your people a chance to really participate in the change will reap rewards.

- Demystify technology. New technology can frighten people who have been doing things the same way for a long time. Find ways to break down the new technology into simple terms. Bring experts in to show your employees how, why and where the new technology fits into the employees' and the company's future.

## Understand Why People Resist Change

No matter how much you communicate, some, perhaps many, people will resist change. It is part of the natural order of things. You can deal with it better if you understand why many people resist—and even fear—change. Here are some of the reasons:

1. **Self-interest.** People fear change will cause them to lose something. For example, when a corporate vice president decided to create a new vice presidency of product development, the existing vice presidents for manufacturing and marketing resisted. They feared losing their rights to approve or veto new product decisions.

2. **Misunderstanding and lack of trust.** When people don't trust the parties initiating change, they suspect hidden, harmful motives. For example, a union opposed one company's proposal of flextime because employees didn't trust the manager who suggested it.

3. **Different assessments.** People view problems from different perspectives. Therefore, they perceive different causes and cures for it. For example, sanitation department employees felt their pick-up delays were due to equipment breakdowns, so they resented it when the city replaced their supervisor instead.

4. **Low tolerance for change.** Sometimes people resist change simply because they fear they'll be unable to competently handle the new conditions. This is particularly true when people must learn new technology. For example, when the accounting department at a major company converted to an accounting software, there was a lot of fear that the change would mess up a system that worked.

4. **Social arrangements.** Efforts to make changes in an organization can flop if they interfere with "cherished social arrangements." For example, executives at an automobile plant proposed staggering the starting and quitting times for different departments in order to decrease traffic congestion. They were surprised when workers objected violently. Many employees had been driving to work together in car-pools for years. The staggered-time proposal threatened these personal relationships.

Regardless of whether change is positive, you must be prepared for people who resist it. Confront their resistance by understanding exactly what it means, responding in ways that help you predict coming events and, most of all, preparing your staff to adapt quickly. How you deal with change is one thing management uses as a yardstick to measure your effectiveness. Confronting and preparing for change are the keys. Stay focused on those, and you'll get through it. And so will your staff.

## Summary

- To be effective, you must manage your time and stress wisely.

- One of the best ways to lessen your stress and manage your time better is to reduce complexity. Look for ways to simplify the work your department does.

- You can reduce a lot of stress in your department by recognizing signs of trouble and confronting them in a straightforward manner.

- Change is a stressor that most likely will make demands on you and your staff and that will be difficult to control.

- Understanding why people resist change and learning ways to help people cope better can improve the chances everyone will be more successful at implementing new ideas and methods.

Chapter 4

# Handling
# People

## What you'll learn:

- How to help new employees get started right.

- How to provide training that gets the job done.

- How to handle common employee problems.

The way you handle the people you supervise is one of the largest factors in your success or failure as a supervisor. When you become a supervisor, you must relate to people in a different way. The way they relate to you changes, too. You've suddenly gone from the audience to center stage. You not only have to gain the respect of your subordinates, you also must gain the respect of your superiors. The way you handle the people on your staff is the biggest key to gaining that respect.

## Orienting the New Employee

How you handle a new employee in the first few weeks on the job can mean the difference between that person's success and failure. Proper orientation determines how quickly the newly hired person can be productive and truly pull her weight in your department.

Too often, busy supervisors overlook orienting new employees. They delegate it to people who are too busy to care or leave it entirely to the human resources department. This is a mistake because the first few days of employment provide you maximum opportunity to quickly make a new employee feel like part of your team. Here's a checklist:

1. **Welcome the employee.** Let the employee know she's a welcome addition to your staff and you're sure she'll do a great job.

2. **Outline the company's objectives.** Show the employee how her job fits into the goals and objectives of the company.

3. **Explain how the company works.** Tell her about the organization's operations, the levels of authority and interrelationships. If you don't have a diagram of this, make one or have it made. Give the employee a copy in her orientation package.

4. **Describe the company's products.** If possible, show the employee examples of the company's products. Use a production flowchart and have actual products on hand to show her.

5. **Tell the employee who the competition is.** Explain what the organization is doing to stay ahead and how she fits in the company's efforts to meet and beat the competition.

6. **Give a brief history of the company.** Show the employee where she fits into the big picture.

7. **Outline what you expect of the employee.** Let her know what you expect from her in terms of her productivity, attitude, reliability, initiative, emotional maturity, teamwork and personal appearance. Make sure she understands how you'll measure her performance against these standards.

8. **Detail the job functions and responsibilities.** Explain your expectations and the criteria for performance appraisals.

9. **Outline the conditions of employment.** If there is a probationary period, tell the employee what you expect during this time. Be clear about working hours, punctuality, attendance, conduct, overtime, termination causes and procedures.

10. **Explain pertinent rules, regulations, policies and procedures.** If you give an employee a manual to read, check back with her to be sure she understands what's included. Don't assume she's read it or understands it.

11. **Introduce the employee to her co-workers.** Take the employee to the place she'll be working. Introduce her to fellow workers and explain what everyone's jobs and responsibilities are.

12. **Review promotion opportunities.** Tell the new employee what criteria you use to determine when she's ready for greater responsibilities.

13. **Explain the benefits.** Make sure the new employee knows when pay periods are, what the salary will be, what insurance benefits and sick time she has, how often she can take breaks, etc. If your company offers recreation facilities, social activities, educational benefits, pensions, etc., tell the new employee about them or provide her with written information.

14. **Explain safety policies.**

15. **Leave the new employee in good hands.** When you take the new employee to her desk, assign an experienced employee to show her where things are and generally look after her. This

shouldn't take long. It may be wise to have several people share this task, particularly if the new employee's tasks overlap those of others in the department. Check back often in the first few weeks to see that the employee is catching on to her job.

Be careful about using words or product jargon the employee won't understand. Use simple, direct language. Check for understanding frequently. Try having employees tell you in their own words what you've just told them.

If you follow these guidelines or delegate them to a trusted employee, you'll save yourself a lot of headaches and wasted time. The employee will appreciate knowing what's expected and will be able to avoid making mistakes. A well-informed employee will be more productive.

## Train Your Staff for Success

We're moving from a skill-based workforce to a knowledge-based workforce. If the people who report to you don't have the skills to do the job, don't throw them away like worn-out tires. "Retread" them with new knowledge! Admittedly there will be some who can't or won't be retrained, but most are waiting for an opportunity. Training is both a practical approach and a socially responsible solution.

The rule of thumb followed by knowledgeable organizations is every dollar spent on training returns three to the bottom line. However, it's important for the supervisor requesting training dollars to clearly show how these dollars will benefit the company in measurable ways. The key word is "measurable." Make sure you connect training and its results to the bottom line. Measure the results.

When you plan training for your employees, take into account how adults learn. The Chinese philosopher Confucius wrote: "I hear and I forget; I see and I remember; I do and I understand." Modern learning principles are based on the following concepts:

1. A person must be motivated to learn. The greater the motivation, the easier it is to learn.

2. The more often we see, hear and do something, the better we're able to remember it.

3. We tend to associate the things we learn with things we already know. If you relate what you're teaching to something the person already knows, he'll learn more easily.

Most of our learning occurs through the five senses: sight, hearing, taste, touch and smell. The more sensory the situation, the more easily learning occurs.

Within a department or group, training without application is a bad investment and generally a waste of time. For the best retention of knowledge, application should begin during the training class and be transferred directly to the point of application, such as an assembly line.

Training must relate to what you, the supervisor, or your employees do on the job. Supervisors must ensure the person designing training courses creates materials that are directly applicable to the work environment.

Don't forget that we learn by doing. No typist ever hit 100 words per minute by watching other typists. Assemblers don't become efficient by watching other assemblers, and a supervisor won't facilitate the perfect meeting by attending other meetings as a participant. The real skill comes from doing. With these concepts in mind, follow these tips for effective training:

- Keep the training area as far away from the frenzy of plant or office operations as possible. Formal training should not take place on the shop floor. The instructor should follow up by helping students apply what they have learned in the classroom.

- Don't allow any beepers or cell phones in the classroom. Once you've closed the door to the classroom, there should be no interruptions.

- Limit sessions to 30 minutes, centered around a concept with a natural break point.

- Remember: Learning is a process, not a destination. Learning doesn't end when the course ends.

- Gain buy-in and ownership for the training. Be sure your manager supports the training before you begin. It's a good idea to have a senior manager address the first training session, telling people why the training is needed and what is expected of employees. Management involvement at the highest level possible is important.

## On-the-Job Training

Many companies leave the training of new employees to their supervisors or co-workers. This isn't the best way, but if it's how training is commonly done at your company, do it as effectively and completely as possible.

If you don't do the training yourself, select someone who has proven he has the ability both to do the work and to pass on the skill to another. Beware of the "Old Joe" syndrome. This occurs when a supervisor says, "Go spend some time with Old Joe. He's been here 30 years. He's done it all; he knows where everything is." The trouble is Old Joe may not know everything, and he may even have acquired bad work habits that he thinks are okay because he's been there so long.

Whatever you do, be sure to set aside enough time to cover each step of the new employee's job thoroughly.

Here are some tips for showing someone how to do a new task.

- Put the employee at ease. Tell her how long it took you to learn the task and maybe admit early mistakes. Let her know your expectations are realistic.

- Explain the "why" of the entire process. Relate the job to the bigger picture and explain how it fits in with the other things going on at your work place.

- Find out what the new person already knows. Has she done anything like this before? If she hasn't, use analogies to relate it to something she understands.

- Explain the vocabulary you'll be using. Define all words and acronyms that apply to the task.

- Go through a sample operation at a normal pace so the employee has an idea of the "flow."

- Next, go through the operation much more slowly several times, explaining each step.

- Explain the difficult steps or those susceptible to error. Identify what those errors might be.

- Carefully go over quality considerations and measurements. Explain roughly what quantities are expected. However, don't set numerical targets at this point.

- Go through the process again and ask the new employee to explain the steps as she understands them. Continue doing this until the new person shows a good understanding of the process.

After you've thoroughly trained the individual, you'll want to see her actually apply what she's learned. Don't take the employee's word that she understands. This isn't about doubting her, it's about being responsible. Often employees will be too shy or nervous to admit they don't understand. To test their performance, follow these steps:

- Have the new employee go through the task slowly, explaining what she's doing at each step.

- Go through the process again, correcting any errors and showing the employee the more difficult steps.

- Have the employee do the task, gradually building confidence. Stress the need for quality over speed.

- As soon as the new employee can do the job, let her do it, but remain ready to help.

After you leave her on her own or under the supervision of another employee, your task still isn't finished. Always check back and review the employee's performance. Be certain she really understands what her job is. Be available if she has questions or needs help.

As the employee gains skill, gradually decrease supervision, checking the work from time to time for quality and productivity. Be sure to correct bad work patterns before they become a habit. Be generous with your praise. Encourage the employee to work independently.

## Mentoring

Some companies use a mentor program. This involves a a trainee and an experienced person who provides guidance. Through mentoring the employee learns not only the ins and outs of the business, he also sees first-hand the long-term potential of a career with the company.

Whatever training technique you use, determine what your employee knows and what he wants to know. Training has such broad, positive effects on employees, it's hard to measure the extent of the benefits.

There is so much you, the supervisor, can do to make the environment you control run smoothly, to create harmony among your workers and to keep production and quality high. Attain all of the success and rewards you— and the people who work for you—deserve.

Think back to your first job and then answer the following questions:

1. Did your supervisor make you feel glad to be there?
2. What kind of training did you receive?
3. What kind of training do you wish you would have received?
4. What kinds of mistakes did you make?
5. Could they have been avoided with better training?
6. What would have been most helpful to you during the first days on your first job? (More hands-on training? More guidance from your co-workers? More written procedures?)
7. What was your biggest fear when you started your job?
8. What helped you overcome that fear?
9. Based on your experience, what is the number-one thing you want to do for new employees when they come to work for you?

## The Power of Recognition

Resentment, low morale, slow-downs, errors, endless gossip, absenteeism and unexplained illness are all signs that you, or management in general, have been taking your employees for granted. Neglecting to give employees a well-deserved pat on the back or some other form of recognition is the greatest cause of bad morale in companies. When it comes to recognition, you know what you want. Your people want it, too.

Here are some ways that you can recognize your employees' hard work.

**Earned praise.** To praise people for routine things, such as showing up for work, is counterproductive. An employee knows when he's done something special. When you see or hear of something exceptional a worker has done, respond as soon as possible and thank that person in specific terms, preferably in front of his co-workers.

**Recognition for performance.** Whenever possible, match the recognition to performance achieved. For example, if the person has stayed late to finish an important project, give him time off. Again, do it publicly. The rule of thumb here is praise publicly and punish privately.

**Respect.** Rodney Dangerfield is a popular comedian who's built a career on saying, "I get no respect!" A lot of people feel they can identify with that. Few people get the respect they need in life. Work is often the only possible place they can achieve some measure of respect. So show respect for employees' knowledge and skills by deferring to their judgment as much as possible when discussing their work.

**Equal treatment.** Be fair. When a team has successfully completed a problem-solving project, realize that all members seldom contribute equally. If there's a reward, how do you share it? Whenever possible, involve the people receiving the reward in that decision.

**Rewards for work well-done.** Survey after survey has shown money is not the number-one reward people want. There's a big difference between compensation and reward. Compensation or pay is the company's exchange with the employee for a set quantity and quality of work. Rewards are for work or achievement above and beyond what's expected.

**Tangible evidence of recognition.** Beyond the appropriate "thank you" and "atta girl," there are many ways to show appreciation of superior effort and superior work. Commendation letters, certificates, trophies and the like last a lot longer than money. If possible, present these rewards publicly, using senior management.

---

Being creative about rewarding people for doing a good job is one of the true "perks" of being a supervisor! In fact, it's best to come up with many different ways to recognize good work. Following are some ideas to stimulate your creativity. At the bottom of the page, write some ideas of your own.

- Let employees recognize each other. Reward an employee with a trophy, plaque or some other object, with the understanding that this person will pass it on when she feels a co-worker deserves recognition.

- Be a cookie elf. Let your employees know how much you appreciate their efforts by leaving cookies wrapped with bright bows on their desks before they get to work.

- Give employee rewards special names. Instead of giving people an "Employee of the Month" award, induct them into the "Movers and Shakers Club" or give the "Rocky Championship" award for succeeding in the face of great odds.

**Your Ideas**

_____

_____

_____

---

# Types of Rewards and Incentives

There are three types of rewards and incentives that are effective.

**1. Informal rewards.** These include anything from saying "thank you" to taking a successful team to lunch at a favorite restaurant. Be spontaneous when handling informal rewards and do it as soon as possible.

**2. Rewards for specific achievements.** When employees meet and exceed some standard, whether it's a sales quota, production targets or quality measures, they should be rewarded for their achievement. These can be rotating awards, a trophy or a plaque that the winners display in their work area for a period of time. It's also a good idea to publicly announce these rewards in the company newspaper or on the bulletin board. Rewards can also be given for unique individual achievement. How you reward your employees is a matter of budget and imagination. The important thing is not to overlook them.

**3. Formal awards.** These are usually presented for efforts made over some predetermined period of time, such as sales representative of the month or year.

Here are some guidelines for effectively rewarding and recognizing these employees:

- Match the reward to the person. Start with her personal preferences; reward her in ways she truly appreciates. For instance, if her hobby is rug weaving, buy her a nicely packaged assortment of yarns. Such rewards may be personal or official, informal or formal, public or private, and they may be gifts or activities, such as a night at the theater. As a supervisor it is useful to survey your people about what they want for rewards and incentives. Survey yourself, too. You also deserve recognition.

- Match the reward to the achievement. Consider the significance of the achievement. Obviously an employee who completes a two-year project ahead of schedule should be rewarded in a more substantial way than someone who does a favor for you.

- Be timely and specific. Give rewards as soon as possible. Rewards that come weeks or months later do little to motivate employees to repeat their actions. Always explain why the award is being given.

Rewards and recognition programs require preparation, planning and effective implementation. If you plan them well and select people who will see them through, you'll increase their effectiveness considerably.

These programs should reflect the company's values and business strategy. Also, as much as possible, employees should participate in the development and execution of the programs. Try to have as much variety as possible in the rewards that you offer. And, most of all, remember, rewards should be given publicly.

Keep in mind that reward programs have a short life span and should be changed frequently. Somewhere on your weekly "to do" list should be activities geared toward recognizing and rewarding your people.

When employees work hard, do their very best, want the company to succeed, and stay late without being asked, it can be very discouraging to them if no one ever says "thank you" or acknowledges their efforts. There's no question that lowered morale means lowered productivity.

Remember this when employees are not operating at their full potential. Find ways to personally acknowledge your employees, whether you give a "Super Employee" plaque or just say "thanks." By doing this, you'll receive some rewards of your own.

Rewarding your employees doesn't take a lot of time, particularly if you allow your people to participate in the process. When rewarding your employees, ask yourself:

1. Are you using a blanket approach? Unless you're rewarding a team, treat people as individuals. The key word here is "individual."

2. Have you said "thanks" and meant it? Recognition can't be casual. It's not something you can do subconsciously. You must be there; you must make personal contact and communicate your gratitude. There's never enough thanks expressed in the world, and yours can make a difference.

3. Do you think you have to reward with money? You don't have to hand out money to effectively acknowledge people's efforts. Surveys have shown that supervisors personally congratulating employees is a more desirable reward than money.

4. Have you looked for effective forms of acknowledgment and recognition that don't cost anything at all? Ask the president to send a handwritten note on her stationery that personally acknowledges an employee's work. Or name a quality improvement after the team or individual that created it.

5. Have you used your imagination? There are many ways to acknowledge good work. For example, you might want to develop a "Behind the Scenes" award for those who seldom receive recognition.

# Ways to Help Employees Improve

With the move toward more and more "knowledge workers" in the workplace, the performance of employees who are required to do many tasks at higher skill levels must be measured by a more comprehensive ruler than ever before. Filling out the standard appraisal form just is not enough.

Under the old system, the supervisor handled a number of management/employee appraisal activities that were treated separately. These activities, which are listed below, were together called the appraisal process.

- Provide feedback to the employee concerning job performance.

- Give data on subjective qualities that don't necessarily relate directly to job performance.

- Assess the data from the appraisal to adjust compensation, bonuses and promotions.

- Provide an opportunity for the supervisor to communicate with the employee.

- Allow the supervisor to give direction about all aspects of the worker's employment.

- Satisfy the legal requirements of Equal Employment Opportunity and Affirmative Action laws.

- Assess employee training needs.

When the supervisor or manager used one performance appraisal to accomplish all of the above, it failed miserably. There were almost no winners and far too many losers. The biggest loser was the company.

All of these activities need to be done, but not in an hour just once a year. You can't do an adequate job when you spend so little time on something this important. The employee deserves better.

Your first concern in conducting an appraisal is determining if the employee's performance is satisfactory. An importance source of information that's often overlooked is customers. Call clients and ask how they think an employee they have contact with is doing. Add their suggestions to your list However, be sure to get data from more than one customer.

Another important source of information about a person's performance is a work group that interacts with the employee. Look for feedback like, "Keeps schedules, meets deadlines, completes units of work, provides hassle-free delivery of products, and produces quality products."

Suppliers and vendors can also give you valuable information about an employee's performance. Your company's success is largely dependent on efficient delivery of goods and services from these suppliers. Therefore, an employee should treat suppliers with the same care she would a customer.

You can obtain this information when you're conducting other business with customers, vendors and employees. Take notes on comments that are made or answers you receive to your questions. Put your notes in the employee's personnel file as you receive them. Don't wait until a few days before the employee's review to begin soliciting information. Not only will it take time to call people to specifically ask them about the employee's performance, but you won't get as true a "read" if people know their responses are being used for an appraisal. It may require a little extra time to take notes and file them after conversations, but by doing this, you'll save more time in the long run.

## The appraisal meeting

After you've gathered information about the employee's overall performance, you're ready to conduct an appraisal meeting. Reserve plenty of time for the meeting, even the entire afternoon. Hold the meeting in a nonthreatening place, where you assume the role of adviser, not warden. And don't forget you should ask questions and listen much more than you should talk. Here are the items that you should cover during this meeting.

- Review the data received from all sources and look for agreement and/or disagreement.

- Find ways to ease, enhance or improve all aspects of the employee's work.

- Set short- and long-term goals for improvement. Don't forget these are the employee's targets as well as yours. Where appropriate, establish time-lines and dates. Take a proactive approach to improvement and show you're interested in the employee's future.

- Arrange for the employee to give you interim progress reports on these goals.

- Accentuate the positives and approach the negatives from the viewpoint that they can be improved upon.

## The personal enhancement meeting

The personal enhancement meeting generally centers on qualitative issues, such as attitude problems, insensitivity to ethnic or gender issues, or other difficulties with a specific worker. If you're not comfortable handling this meeting, ask your human resources representatives if they have been trained for this sort of thing.

This meeting should take an hour or less, unless there are unusual problems. The key is to treat this meeting as a separate event. Don't confuse it with an appraisal meeting.

## The training enhancement meeting

Every employee needs and deserves to have this meeting with you. For the knowledge worker, this is extremely important. There are a number of things you can do to make the meeting a success.

- Become very familiar with the employee's training history. It's important for you to have a copy of each employee's training record. If no files exist, create them and see that they're maintained.

- Become familiar with the worker's formal schooling, company-sponsored courses, on-the-job training, adult education classes or on-going university work.

- Don't discount courses that may not relate specifically to the employee's job classification. All education is useful when added to the whole. In some cases, you may need to determine if a worker actually reads.

- During the meeting, get the employee's ideas on what training will make her more effective. Find out how the employee sees herself as part of the company and how training can help with that.

- Develop a short- and long-term training enhancement plan. Include a schedule and timeline and give the employee a copy. Check back often to see if targets are being met and if the training meets the employee's needs. Find ways to measure how the training is affecting the employee's performance.

- Last, include funds for training in your budget. Be a powerful advocate for your people's training with upper management. When they look good, you look good.

Employee evaluations don't have to be a dreaded event. They can be a time of discovery for both you and the employee. Use the following checklist to determine how you can make evaluations more positive for both you and your staff.

1. Why does your company currently conduct employee evaluations?

2. What would you like to achieve by evaluating your employees?

3. What's the current payoff for the employee being evaluated?

4. What benefits would you like for your employees to gain from a performance evaluation?

5. How can you change the evaluation process so it becomes nonthreatening and even fun? Use your imagination!

6. What are some benefits you think employees should receive from being evaluated that they currently aren't receiving?

## Identifying Candidates for Promotion

Not long ago, if you lasted a few years on the job, didn't get into serious trouble and had a modicum of intelligence, you would probably receive some sort of promotion. This is much less likely today. Employees are being asked to take more responsibility, know more about their work and have special skills that didn't even exist 25 years ago. The move toward team-based organizations is a good example of this. In this environment, the supervisor must have different standards for recommending an employee for promotion.

There are several criteria that will help you make the right promotions. These employees should have experience or skills in these areas:

- Participation in and facilitation of problem-solving and project specific teams. This is valuable because it demonstrates several of the qualities most desirable in a supervisor.

- Knowledge of problem-solving skills.

- Ability to work toward consensus.

- Effective communication skills.

- Customer involvement. The ability to deal with customers successfully is a valuable quality in an employee. The more responsibility employees get, the more contact they're likely to have with customers.

Here are other questions you should consider in making your decision.

- Does the employee handle his work in an orderly way, meeting deadlines and completing assignments?

- Does the employee show initiative in acquiring additional job skills? Is the employee trainable?

- Does the employee assume leadership when it's needed in the workplace?

- Is the employee familiar with new technology, including computers, electronic mail and various software applications?

- Does the employee have good writing and presentation skills?

The key to improving the appraisal process is to stop using it as a catch-all. You can't do an adequate job when you spend an hour talking about an entire year of an employee's work. When possible, base pay and pay increases on the employee's value to the company, always making sure the employee has an attainable way to increase that value. If you follow the simple steps outlined here, you can do honest and fair appraisals that reflect the true capabilities and potential of your employees.

Identifying good candidates for promotion is an important part of a supervisor's job. Think about the following questions in terms of how you are "growing" the supervisors of tomorrow for your company:

1. Do you make it a part of your job to understand your company's plans for the future and convey those plans to all of your staff members so they can prepare for that future too?

2. Do you give every person on your staff an opportunity to "shine" rather than giving the plum assignments to the same people again and again?

3. Do you take the time to help your employees improve the skills you know they need to be promoted, such as presentation skills, written communication skills, etc.?

4. Do you make sure other supervisors and upper management are aware of the contributions of individuals on your staff?

5. Have you established an atmosphere that allows employees to talk to you openly about their goals for future success?

# Handling Problem Employees

Being a supervisor requires you to do a lot more than simply order people around. You need to be a counselor, confessor, mediator, cop, parent—you name it. Common sense will solve most of your problems and situations. For the few you can't handle, the company may have a specialist.

If you do get in over your head, don't put off doing something and don't be afraid to ask for help. Almost every manager and supervisor has been where you are.

If an employee comes to you with a personal problem, don't be too quick to send her to the company's counselor or human resources expert. You're the first line of defense and a little compassion and patient listening may be all that's needed. Remember, however, you're not a therapist.

Here's a list of early warning signs that can alert you if a worker is having problems or facing difficulties that might impact your team and its productivity.

- Unexcused absences
- Unexcused tardiness
- Violations of the law
- Possessing or using illegal drugs on the premises
- Leaving work without permission
- Safety violations
- Dress code violations
- Garnishment of wages
- Insubordination
- Fighting
- Reduced productivity
- Making mistakes
- No interest in training

No one enjoys having to deal with problem employees. Here's a checklist to help you during the times you have to get tough on bad behavior.

1. Be sure everyone on your staff is aware of your expectations about behavior.

2. When an employee fails to meet your expectations, tell her immediately (and privately). Be specific and address the behavior, not the person.

3. Don't carry a grudge or assume the worst if a person behaves badly. Remain unemotional and treat it as a business problem, not a personal problem.

4. Follow the steps your company has established for disciplining employees. Make sure the employee understands what's involved and the seriousness of the actions you must take.

5. Be alert to honest attempts to improve her behavior. Don't write the person off and simply go through the motions until you can fire her or force her to leave. It's usually cheaper to rehabilitate the people you have than to train someone new.

Here are some recommendations for handling problem employees.

1. Talk to the person about the problem privately. Taking anyone to task in front of peers is humiliating and extraordinarily destructive.

2. Be very specific about the problem. Saying something like, "You're not shaping up," won't help. Instead say, "You came to work on Monday smelling of liquor and dressed differently. What's going on?"

3. Be willing to listen. Giving advice is optional. Remember, you're not a trained substance-abuse

counselor. However, it's good to know where to refer an employee who's having problems.

4. Know what help is available and where to find it. If the employee gives you a lot of flak and defensive behavior, that's a strong indicator a problem exists. A guilty person is likely to attack whoever confronts her with the problem, whether it's drugs, or other negative behavior.

5. Realize you're there to help. Be willing to go the extra mile to see the individual gets help. Don't react to an employee's anger. Most of the time it's not really directed toward you

6. If performance is the problem, be sure the "system" isn't at fault. If the employee is using a machine that can't maintain the required quality or precision, there's nothing she can do about it. Again, be specific about the performance you want improved. Find out what you can do to help. Is more training required? Is the employee a square peg in a round hole? It may be appropriate to arrange a schedule to work on the improvements you expect from the employee.

7. When you have to discipline, be sure the employee knows the rules. Termination is truly the last resort. But when it's necessary, don't shrink from it. Other employees are aware of bad behavior, and they won't respect you if you let it continue.

## Monitoring Employees' Progress

When you give direction, set policy, establish a plan or schedule of activities with an employee, you must follow up periodically. After you get to know your employees, you will recognize which ones you can trust to handle things on their own and which ones require monitoring. Either way, you should expect compliance and make sure that it occurs. Try these suggestions:

- Document the employee's performance. Look for improvement and any problems the employee is having.

- Accentuate the positive. When you see improvement, be quick to say something about it.

- Don't ignore performance problems just because the person is involved in a company-assistance program. By this time, you should have informed the employee of the options and he should know what to expect.

- Always protect the confidentiality of the employee's personal problems as well as his participation in an assistance program.

In summary, when handling a problem employee:

1. Be fair and direct.
2. Discipline and counsel in private.
3. Don't delay taking action.
4. Know where to get professional help for specific kinds of problems.
5. Accentuate the positive.
6. Be sure to follow up on the progress of counseling and monitor improvements in performance.

If you do these things quickly and thoroughly, you'll reduce problems with the worker considerably.

## Absenteeism and Tardiness

Absenteeism is one of those corporate or departmental health measures that's often overlooked. Absenteeism may be a symptom of a deeper underlying illness. Before you resort to drastic measures, assess the general morale of your group or department. If there's a "cancer" in your group or organization, you won't cure it by shouting at it. Get at the heart of the real problem.

To limit absenteeism, you must have an attendance policy. Make sure the employee understands regular attendance is required. The policy should state that advance notice of an absence be given when possible. Make sure employees know who to notify. Generally, it's their immediate supervisor.

Let employees know of their importance in accomplishing company and departmental goals. Emphasize how the work of the organization suffers when they're absent.

If there's a problem, address the issue. Require all employees who have been absent to report to you before starting work. This gives you a chance to discover the real reasons for the absence and counsel the employee.

Keep records. Maintain an individual record for each worker that shows all absences, their length, the dates of notification and the reasons.

Allow time for personal business. Employees sometimes feel compelled to call in sick so they can take care of personal business that can be handled only during work hours. Under the condition that advance notice be given, it's a good idea to allow your workers a certain amount of time off to handle personal business. At the same time, keep a record of this, too.

Tardiness can become a habit if not handled early on. It's important to confront the employee immediately and determine whether the tardiness was avoidable. Keep records of this the same way you would for absenteeism. Chronic late-comers should be made aware of the seriousness of the situation and agree to a plan to remedy the problem. If the tardiness continues, be prepared to take disciplinary action.

Today's more flexible lifestyle, work environment and even cultural differences sometimes make it difficult to enforce strict time guidelines. As the supervisor, you must determine what's acceptable and then declare your standards out loud and in writing. Then, enforce them. Hit and miss enforcement won't do.

## The Supervisor and the Labor Contract

If you're a supervisor in a unionized organization, you have a dual responsibility. First, you must work toward achieving maximum productivity from workers. Second, as a member of management, you must be aware of and adhere to management's commitments under the union contract, even if you don't agree with some points. The organization is accountable for the supervisor's failure to uphold the agreements between management and the union.

The Labor Relations Act, passed in 1947, outlines unfair labor practices affecting the supervisor. These include legal and actionable offenses that could bring about your dismissal and a great deal of trouble and expense to your company. Don't treat them casually. The main issues are:

1. Blocking employee efforts to form or join a union.
2. Attempting to influence a labor union.
3. Discriminating against the members of a union.
4. Discriminating against a worker who brings a charge against a management employee under the Labor Management Relations Act.

## The Grievance Process

It's often advantageous to settle a grievance at the supervisory level. It boosts management's confidence in the supervisor, fosters an atmosphere of cooperation without costly arbitration and prevents minor problems from becoming major ones that hurt morale and cause disruption.

Unusual situations or grievances that affect a large number of employees should go to a higher management level or to the personnel department. In any case, the supervisor should never try to block the grievance process.

Following are steps in a typical grievance procedure:

1. The worker, the union steward and the supervisor discuss the grievance.
2. The grievance is discussed by the supervisor's superior and the union grievance committee.
3. The union grievance committee, the manager of the local organization and its industrial relations manager evaluate the grievance.
4. The grievance is discussed by the union grievance committee, the organization's top general management, industrial relations manager and national union representatives.
5. The grievance is discussed by top management and national union representatives.
6. The grievance is referred to a mutually agreed-upon arbitrator for final resolution.

To avoid most grievance problems, develop an understanding of labor law, the union contract, past accepted practice and your responsibilities as a supervisor. Promote a good working relationship with the union steward. Create as fair a working environment as possible. Keep an open mind and encourage discussion of problems. Investigate the cause of each complaint. Evaluate the facts surrounding the issue. Determine a course of action to remedy the problem. Advise all people affected by your solution before implementing it. Follow up on the results and side effects of the solution.

The best solution to grievance problems is to uncover conditions that have the potential to become "situations" and deal with them. Don't wait for something to happen.

## Supervising Minority Workers

The term minority worker refers to an employee who is a member of a certain ethnic, age or handicapped group. Female employees may be considered minority workers, depending on the industry.

As a supervisor, you must know the laws relating to minority workers. Most companies have documents issued by the human resources department.

Issues that arise because of discrimination are negative, rob you of energy and are self-defeating. You must take an active approach in this area and never let it come up in the first place. It's better to come to work with the viewpoint that all of your people have something to offer. See diversity as a positive.

## Creating an Atmosphere of Equality

Be aware of your organization's policies and practices that have resulted from Equal Employment Opportunity and Affirmative Action regulation. Learn to recognize and eliminate stereotyping and preconceptions that may exist within your company or department. Provide clear, challenging and achievable expectations for all of your employees. Provide training support and encouragement that fit individual needs. Be aware of and sensitive to issues that commonly arise in workforces composed of different groups. Help facilitate understanding and tolerance among all employees. Communicate regularly with your employees to minimize isolation and maximize the contributions of everyone. Provide excellent feedback on performance for all employees.

Hopefully, this will be what it should be: a nonissue. If, for any reason, it does become a problem, get all the facts. Then be as honest and forthcoming as possible. Again, the best solution is a proactive one. Head off these difficulties before they have a chance to start.

## Summary

- Develop and follow a specific plan for orienting new employees to your department.

- Don't try to evaluate all of an employee's performance issues in one appraisal meeting. Have several meetings to address specific areas of performance, including personal enhancement and training needs.

- When dealing with problem employees, talk to them in private and be very specific about what you perceive to be a problem. Be willing to listen, but don't hesitate to refer them to an outside counselor if their problems are beyond your ability to handle.

- When you must discipline an employee, check periodically to be sure that your directions are being followed. If absenteeism and tardiness are a problem, be sure everyone knows what your policies are and what the consequences to expect.

- Try to deal with conflict in a win-win manner. It's also acceptable to be dominant or accommodating or even to avoid the conflict in specific situations. You must be the judge.

- You must be especially concerned about creating a fair, equitable working environment. Be knowledgeable of the labor laws as they apply to your situation. Remember that if you treat others as you want to be treated and demand the same of those who work for you, you won't go wrong.

# Chapter 5

# Communication and Team-Building

## What you'll learn:

- How to take responsibility for the communication you send and receive.
- How to build more productive teams through effective communication.
- How to develop the communication skills to defuse conflict and build harmony.

Of all the elements the supervisor needs to be successful, communication offers the highest chance for success or failure. In hundreds of surveys at different companies, employees cite poor communication as the greatest source of wasted time, effort and material as well as internal and external conflict. Good communication skills are essential for effectively supervising others, and they also determine how well your staff works together as a team.

## Types of Communication

There are many different ways we communicate with each other, including:

- Conversation, orders and presentations
- Written reports, memos and plans

- Phone calls and phone messages
- E-mail
- Faxes

Given the number and kinds of communications a supervisor must send and receive in the course of a day, the opportunities to succeed or fail are too numerous to count.

The key point is you must take responsibility for your communication, whether you send it or receive it. You may ask how you can be responsible for communications you receive. The answer is simple: The majority of people are not good communicators, and to have any level of communication at all, you have to take responsibility. Because we can only control our own responsibility, we have to start with ourselves.

You can take on more responsibility for the communication you receive by following these guidelines:

- Don't take anything for granted. Don't assume the data you receive is correct until you check it, especially if it's from someone you don't know well or who previously provided incorrect information.

- Verify instructions you're not sure of. You won't be considered incompetent if you ask for more explanation of something you don't understand.

- Teach your employees to communicate more effectively with you. Let people know what you expect. Don't expect your employees to read your mind. Show them and, whenever possible, give them written step-by-step procedures to follow.

- Never accept verbal information when you really need it in writing. All too often, verbal communication is accepted when a written form is more appropriate. Remember the old game where you whisper something in one person's ear and he repeats it to the next person and so on. By the time the message reaches the last person, it generally isn't even close to the original. The same thing happens to companies that rely heavily on verbal communication. The message moves through several layers of people until it's not recognizable. This problem can cost your company millions in errors, rework, missed orders and schedules.

• Be an excellent listener. Make sure you are not too busy talking to hear something important.

Take a moment and think about your personal communication skills, then answer the following questions:

1. What are your strongest communication skills?

2. What are your weakest communication skills?

3. How could you be more effective if you improved in the areas where you're weak?

4. What rewards do you think you would gain from improving your communication skills?

5. What communication skills that you don't have now would you need in order to reach your career goals?

6. Where can you go to get the skills you need?

You can become responsible for your communications by doing the following:

- Be brief and clear in your conversations and written communications. Like you, your workers are very busy.

- Be honest, but don't use honesty to belittle others. You've probably met people who say things like, "I'm going to be brutally frank." This is someone who uses truth as a weapon to hurt or destroy others. It does no good to tell someone he isn't bright enough to be promoted. You can, however, take a positive approach and suggest training or something special to enhance an employee's ability. You can be honest and kind. These aren't mutually exclusive concepts.

- Put as many of your communications in writing as possible. The ANVO system (Accept No Verbal Orders) can help you survive a hectic workplace.

- If your writing skills are weak, improve them. There are many courses designed especially for business people. When you master these skills, your superiors will notice.

- Learn to give good presentations. This is a skill that marks a good, promotable supervisor.

- Give your complete attention to those who communicate with you.

- Eliminate unnecessary jargon. If you use too much jargon, you can annoy the people you want on your side and risk not being understood.

Don't be discouraged when communications fail for reasons you can't control. By making a conscious effort to improve, you'll learn what works and what doesn't. Strive to be a great communicator, then teach others and make life easier for yourself.

Above all, communicate with your employees. Keeping track of the communication in your department should be as automatic as keeping track of production figures.

---

Check on your communication. Ask yourself if any of the following has happened in the past few weeks.

1. Have you sent any incomplete communications?

2. Have you sent out communications that contained incorrect data?

3. Were communications sent to the wrong person?

4. Were any of your communications delayed or not sent at all?

5. Did people appear to be confused about any of your communications?

6. Did people say they needed more details about what you were communicating?

7. Did people seem to think that some of your communications were irrelevant?

8. Did you send any communications that contained unnecessary emotional content?

**Time to Improve**

If you answered "yes" to one or more of these questions, you have room to improve your communication. Target one area at a time for improvement. Remember, it's always better to err on the side of too much communication than too little!

---

## Communication and Your Customers

Who are your customers? For a long time, "customers" were defined as the people or companies that bought your company's products. Dr. W. Edwards Deming gave us a deeper look at this concept as it relates to communications and the internal customers.

As shown in Figure 5.1, the link between the individual and his or her customers and suppliers is inevitably some form of communication. Therefore, this is where the greatest potential for errors exists.

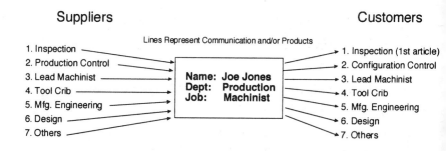

*Figure 5.1. Customer/Supplier Relationship for the Individual*

The customer/supplier relationship exists throughout every organization, whether at the individual, team, department or even divisional level. For instance, Figure 5.2 shows the relationships among departments in a typical manufacturing company. Again, the key to success is through communication.

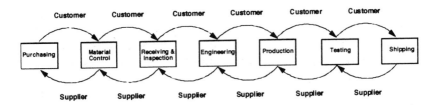

*Figure 5.2. Customer/Supplier Relationship
at the Departmental Level*

In order to communicate effectively with your internal customers, it's essential to:

1. Identify them.

2. Determine what kind of communication they need from you to do their jobs.

3. Determine what kind of communication you need from them for your staff to do their jobs.

4. Develop a communication style that builds bridges instead of walls when you discuss plans and work together.

Once you've identified your internal customers and those who provide customer service to you and your department, all involved must communicate what they need from each other to do their jobs. One way to do this is through meetings.

103

Identify your internal customers by answering these questions from both a personal and departmental standpoint.

1. Who needs input from you or your department before they can do their jobs? (List as many as you can think of.)

2. What do they need?

3. By looking at these people as customers, how can you provide better service to them?

4. Whom do you or your staff need input from in order to do your jobs?

5. What do you need from these people in order to do your job more effectively?

6. If these people viewed you and your department as customers, what could they do to make you feel you were getting better service?

# Communicating through Effective Meetings

How many meetings does your company hold each week, month or year? A couple of hundred a year? More or less? How much time is wasted by these meetings? That's the key question.

Let's do some simple math using as an example a medium-sized company with 10 functional departments and 300 employees.

| Description | Number of Meetings |
|---|---|
| One staff meeting per week per department | 10/wk |
| Special subject meetings | 10/wk |
| Immediate problem meetings | 5/wk |
| Customer meetings | 5/wk |
| Supplier meetings | 5/wk |
| Problem-solving team meetings | 5/wk |
| Miscellaneous meetings | 5/wk |
| **Total Meetings** | **45/wk** |

Assuming a one-hour average per meeting and a 48-week year for businesses, that's a total of 2,160 meetings. If we assume that an average of four people attend each meeting, that's 8,640 production hours that are spent in meetings. Furthermore, if we assume the average cost per person per hour (after adding hourly wage, overhead, general administration and profit) is $75 an hour, this means the total staff cost to hold this company's meetings is $648,000 per year.

Even if the figures were 20 percent lower, this is still a big number. If your meetings are 50-percent productive, which is high for most companies, that's still a lot of dollars. If you want a successful career as a supervisor and to move up the ladder, fix any problems with meetings as quickly as you can.

The question you must ask before holding a meeting is, "Will this meeting add value to the department or company's operations?"

Meetings are generally held to provide information, make decisions, develop plans or solve problems. These activities involve you, the supervisor. As much as you might like to, you can't avoid attending meetings. Therefore, it's beneficial to make your meetings efficient and productive. Here are some key ingredients to effective meetings.

- Determine beforehand whether the meeting is really necessary. Determine if you could communicate more effectively by a phone call, e-mail or memo.

- Carefully decide who should attend the meeting. Be sure everyone there has something relevant to contribute. Under no circumstances should you hold meetings with casts of thousands unless the CEO is delivering a state of the company message to all employees. People who don't have essential roles should be given the option of attending.

- Make sure the purpose of the meeting is clearly understood and agreed to by all those attending.

If you determine a meeting is necessary, follow these ground rules to avoid wasting time.

1. Establish a clear agenda and stick to it.
2. Know when to step in and refocus the group if employees get off the subject.
3. Have someone take notes. You could use a large flipchart or an overhead projector so everyone can see.
4. Assign specific action items to the people attending.

5. Send a follow-up report to all participants within 48 hours of the meeting's conclusion. This report should provide a brief synopsis of the meeting's goals, activities and action items.

6. Start and end the meeting precisely on time.

---

Here's how to put together your meeting agenda.

1. The agenda must be sent in advance.

2. The agenda must include where the meeting will take place and when.

3. The exact business of the meeting and the goals of the person holding the meeting should be stated clearly on the agenda.

4. The agenda should include what the group is expected to accomplish for each item to be discussed.

5. Set time limits for discussing each item on the agenda.

6. Indicate which attendees may leave after their portions of the meeting have been discussed.

7. Inform attendees how they should prepare for the meeting and what materials, if any, they should bring.

---

## Presentations

The ability to make good presentations is a key ingredient for career advancement. When you present well, you gain the respect and support of others. You're seen as being more authoritative. People seek you out and enjoy being around you when you're at ease in front of an audience. And upper management sees you as someone they want to develop as an important representative of the company.

The value of being a good presenter can't be overstated. Because it's such a comparatively rare skill, it's all the more important that you develop your abilities in this area.

However, don't confuse the ability to make excellent presentations with being a great public speaker. The two are miles apart. In fact, making presentations is far easier than most people assume.

The following guidelines will help you turn a mediocre presentation into a stellar one every time.

- Use visuals as much as possible. Studies have shown that the average reading level of employees, including college graduates, is between a 6th- and 8th-grade level. Although you'll have to use words, you'll be much more effective if you intersperse those words with effective graphic images.

- Be thoroughly prepared. Know your subject well. The quickest way to look unprofessional and incompetent is to rush into a meeting at the last minute with a handful of scattered notes to sort out in front of your audience. You don't impress with flash; you impress with preparation, knowledge and a message that's clearly stated.

- Know your audience. What do people need to hear? Remember, you're selling something and the attention span of the buyer is short. Most great salespeople say they know in the first five minutes if they've made the sale. You have to hook your audience, and you have to do it early. If you're presenting to senior execs, that's one audience. If your presentation is to other managers at your own level, that's another audience, and if the audience contains line workers, that's a different audience, too. Plan your presentation accordingly.

- Have a goal for the presentation. Know what you want to accomplish and then gear your presentation toward accomplishing that goal.

- Avoid jargon. Use clear, specific, declarative, short sentences. Back up your assertions with well-researched data. When presenting, leave your opinions behind. Audience members have their own. Convince them instead with facts and well-supported ideas.

Your presentation will always be effective if you follow these basic rules:

1. **Organize your presentation.** Follow the three rules of preview and summary. These are:
   - Tell them what you're going to tell them.
   - Tell them.
   - Tell them what you told them.

2. **Develop a list of key points.** Keep the list in front of you so you don't forget them.

3. **Have a strong opening and closing.** It's worth spending extra time on these critical areas of your presentation. You want to grab the attention of your audience within the first few seconds you begin speaking. And when you close, you want to leave the impression that you're a highly effective, well-organized speaker.

4. **Work from least important to most important.**

5. **Use good supporting materials.** You may use examples, comparisons, quotes and audiovisuals.

Does a fear of public speaking prevent you from developing your presentation skills? If so, you're not alone! Here are some tips to help you feel more at ease when making presentations.

1. Prepare, prepare, prepare. The absolute best defense against anxiety is knowledge. Know your subject inside and out.

2. Visualize yourself doing a good job. See everything going right and people applauding your excellent presentation. Imagine people asking you difficult questions and "see" yourself handling them. Make time to visualize how you want your presentation to go as you prepare for it.

3. Don't be afraid to say "I don't know." If you're asked a question and you don't know the answer, make a note of the question and tell the person that you'll get back to him with an answer.

4. Don't be too critical of yourself. Give yourself a break. If you know someone who gives good presentations, ask him or her to evaluate your presentation and list the areas you need to work on as well as note the things you do well.

5. Vow to talk "with" your audience, not down to them. The information you're trying to convey should hold the audience's interest, not yours.

6. Listen carefully when you're asked a question and never cut off the person. Decide on an answer and be brief. If you don't agree with a point, find a part upon which you can agree.

7. Remember that people want you to succeed. Have fun. You'll survive it, and the gains are certainly worth the effort.

6. **Support your opening.** Use key points and transitions to move from one point to the next. Your points must flow and connect logically.

7. **Summarize with a call to action**. In a way you're asking for the approval of your audience and their agreement on what you're proposing.

# Communication Skills to Build Teams

For many years management was based on what's called a hierarchical structure. Top-down. People in charge, the bosses, made decisions and handed them down to the workers who did what they were told.

The structure was basically a pyramid. At the top was upper management, then middle management, then lower management and finally foremen and workers. Orders filtered down from the top through middle management to the workers at the bottom. The thinking was the people at the top knew everything, and the people at the bottom knew very little.

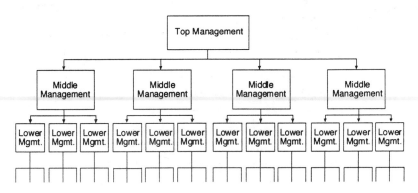

Foreman, Supervisors, Etc.

*Figure 5.3. Hierarchical Management Structure*

This structure was purposely based on individuals reporting to individuals. This created a situation in which the exchange of information and overall objectives were very narrow. Wherever you were in the structure, there was usually just one person to communicate with.

Modern management systems are moving more toward a horizontal structure, where information and ideas reach all people and departments involved in a project. This structure is shown in Figure 5.4.

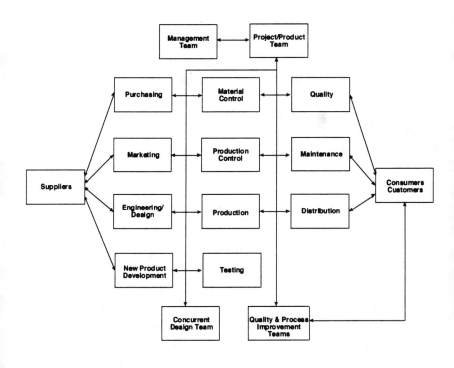

*Figure 5.4. A New Way to View an Organization*

The inherent flaw in the hierarchical system is that it discourages cooperation and communication among departments. In a modern business environment, almost every problem is understood to be cross-functional to some degree. Furthermore, it has been shown time and time again that the best problem-solving approach uses teams representative of all the involved departments working together, to share ideas, information and resources.

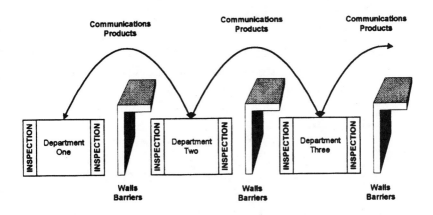

*Figure 5.5. The Team-Building/Problem-Solving Environment*

Today, top management recognizes that employees closest to the real work of a business have the expertise, knowledge, information and viewpoints to make a difference, especially when they work together cooperatively and pool their resources.

Through teams of all kinds and at all levels, employees solve problems, improve processes, develop products, make decisions and, in some cases, manage themselves to make the business work effectively.

113

"Teamwork" is more than a buzzword of the 1990s. Companies that use effective team-building and operating skills have proven they have an advantage over those who don't.

There are several kinds of teams that can be formed for different purposes and directed at different kinds of problems. These include:

- **Management teams.** These teams generally oversee one or more project teams and provide oversight, knowledge, direction of vision, resources and removal of barriers that prevent the project team from meeting its objectives.

- **Concurrent engineering or design teams.** Companies are finally realizing that in addition to the designer, it is a good idea to have employees from quality, maintenance, purchasing and production present throughout the innovation, design and prototype-building phases of a new product. (If you've ever tried to repair something with parts that don't fit, then you'll understand why getting maintenance involved from the beginning is so important.)

- **Cross-functional problem-solving teams.** These came in with TQM (Total Quality Management), and while business has moved on to newer, more jargon-laden management tools, cross-functional teams have remained. Here's where the supervisor is key, not only as a coach and facilitator, but also as a participant. Also, several of your staff may be part of cross-functional problem-solving teams. It's important that you assess their progress and provide them with the incentives and rewards their successes deserve.

- **Process-improvement teams.** These are similar to cross-functional problem-solving teams, but they are usually formed within a department or group and focus on problems that are narrower in scope.

- **Quality circles.** If you have studied the quality revolution that began in Japan in the 1950s, you've undoubtedly heard about quality circles. Essentially, these are problem-solving and process-improvement teams that operate on a continuous basis. Companies that use them have shown that making less dramatic, but continuous incremental improvements to processes, products and services improves business.

Effective teams share several important characteristics:

- A shared purpose, a common goal.

- People who are able to work together.

- An effective mix of skills and strengths.

- An ability to reach consensus.

When you're forming teams, selecting the right people to participate is essential. Qualities you want in a good team member are:

1. **Ability to speak up.** If people won't talk during a meeting, they won't contribute.

2. **A risk-taker.** Although this is not essential, it certainly helps. Part of what you want from a successful team are ideas and the fortitude to try them out.

3. **Strongly motivated.** People assigned to a team against their wishes are likely to be, at best, inactive and, at worst, destructive.

4. **Helpful.** People enjoy helping. Give them a chance to be part of a team, reward their help appropriately, and you can reap extraordinary benefits.

5. **Willing to try.** This is the person who will pitch in and try to make things succeed.

6. **Efficiency.** When you've led several meetings that wander all over the place without really getting anything done, you'll appreciate the efficient person.

7. **Energetic**. All your team members have their regular work assignments. Being energetic is a real plus.

A piece of advice: Don't look for people who always get along and who never make waves. Waves are part of a change. Often in the process of making waves, issues that need to be addressed are put on the table where everyone can examine them. Difficult decisions require the ability to confront the tough issues.

The supervisor must mediate disagreements, get the timid to offer their thoughts and ideas, and keep the team focused on its goals. When a number of competing solutions have been listed, the supervisor must draw the team to want a consensus that everyone can live with. If consensus isn't achieved when a deadline arrives, team members will be strangely missing or have something else to do.

In the end, trust is going to have a lot to do with the team's success or failure. Do team members trust their leader and each other? Trust is built by people who:

- Listen well.

- Consistently meet commitments.

- Bring reliable information to meetings.

- Demonstrate ability.

- Show real interest in other team members.
- Use common sense in their judgments.
- Support the team.

Remember, to establish a team-building environment, there's a lot to overcome. Most of your workers have seen so-called "new approaches" to doing things come and go—mostly go. They're justifiably cynical about management's "flavor of the month" program. As a supervisor, you must help your people set aside the past, begin handling the present, and look toward the future.

## Communication Styles to Manage Conflict

Conflict among employees usually follows a series of stages. It's up to you as the supervisor to be alert for the symptoms and use your communication skills to handle the problem before it affects the entire department. In most cases, conflicts escalate in the following steps:

1. One person wants something, and another person disagrees or obstructs progress.
2. Both parties feel frustrated because they can't do or get what they want.
3. They manifest their frustration by blaming each other.
4. They feel angry and do or say things based on how they've come to interpret what happened.
5. Both parties react, and the conflict escalates.

If you recognize conflict, you can take steps to manage it. These steps depend upon the severity of the conflict and the urgency with which you must resolve it. Each of the following five methods offers ways to get a handle on a potentially destructive situation.

Try the following activities to improve communication in your department.

- Schedule a daily walk-around for the specific purpose of staying in contact with your people. Schedule it late in the morning, after people have had a chance to get into their work.

- Schedule a weekly meeting with work groups within the department. Do this formally. If it only takes 15 minutes, fine, but allow for more time if needed.

- Schedule a monthly sit-down meeting with individual employees, perhaps for a half-hour. Use this time to ask about the status of projects, how they're doing with goals and objectives and training needs.

- Schedule a full departmental meeting every two months. Make it your "state of the department" or "group" meeting. This is the time for recognition, good news, major announcements, promotions, and the like.

**Your Ideas**

Write down some activities you think you could do to improve communication in your department:

_____

_____

_____

_____

_____

_____

_____

# 1. Resolve conflict by being dominant or forceful.

Use this method when there's an emergency, and quick, decisive action is imperative. If these issues are vital to the organization's welfare and you're very sure you're right, you may need to take this approach. With people who take advantage of others, you can't be accommodating. You must view this as destructive to the group and deal with it forcefully.

# 2. Give in and accommodate the other person.

This is a bit like risk-assessment. You have to decide if what you give up will resolve the situation and allow the parties to move forward. Be aware that an obsessive need to be right is a behavior problem. Always try to give the other person room to achieve some degree of rightness, even when you must decide against his position.

Use this method when you may be wrong, or to give way to a better position or to show you can be reasonable. A word of caution: If you can't do this sincerely and it appears to be condescending or nothing more than a ploy, you will lose more than you gain.

This is a good method for handling conflict and maintaining cooperation when issues are much more important to others than you. Do this when harmony and goodwill are essential. You might want to do this to help subordinates grow, even if you know you're right and the other person is going to make a mistake—so long as it's not going to damage the company or cause financial losses.

# 3. Resolve conflict using trade-offs or compromise.

Use this method when your opponent has equal power and you're both committed to mutually exclusive goals. It may be necessary to do this to achieve temporary settlements to complex issues. You can also do this when your goal is important but not worth the effort of being more assertive with a resistant person.

## 4. Resolve conflict by postponing it.

Use this tactic if an issue is trivial or more important issues are pressing. It's also effective when the potential disruption outweighs the benefits of pursuing the matter or when there's potential for fights. By postponing conflict you let people cool down and gain perspective.

## 5. Resolve conflict by finding a "win-win" solution.

The best method for managing conflict is to collaborate, to create a "win-win" or an integrated solution that satisfies both parties. This is especially important when both sides feel too important to compromise. Collaboration is the best way to gain long-term commitment and reach genuine consensus among everyone involved.

Continuing conflicts have a way of forcing people to take sides and pulling in others that originally weren't part of the problem. Therefore, it's important that these conflicts be resolved quickly and with as little leftover bad feelings as possible.

# Summary

- Developing good communication skills is critical to your success as a supervisor. To be a good communicator, you must accept responsibility not only for the messages you send, but also for the messages you receive.

- As a well-rounded, promotable professional, you must develop all of your communication skills, including conducting effective meetings and making interesting, powerful presentations. By focusing on these areas and preparing yourself for success, you'll not only eliminate unproductive meetings, but you'll inspire others to follow your lead.

- Additionally, as a supervisor, you use your communication skills to share information with others in your company and to build stronger, more effective teams.

- And finally, if conflict occurs, you use your communication skills in a way that is most appropriate for the situation. Keep in mind the first choice for resolving conflict is always to create a "win-win" scenario.

Chapter 6

# The Supervisor's Tool Kit

Just because you're a supervisor now doesn't mean you don't use tools. The machinist has a lathe; you have a computer with word processors and spreadsheets.

You also have one of the best tools ever devised—your mind. However, you must feed it with knowledge, adjust it with experience and constantly maintain it with exercise if you want it to serve you well.

There are many fine tools available for the supervisor. Never stop acquiring knowledge. Acquiring new knowledge is your route to faster promotions, greater responsibility and a larger game to play. Make reading and learning a habit. The benefits extend far beyond your job. They can help you—and the people you supervise—lead happier, more productive lives.

# Index